THE
GREAT ROA
TO BATH

THE GREAT ROAD TO BATH

Daphne Phillips

COUNTRYSIDE BOOKS
NEWBURY BERKSHIRE

ISBN 0 905392 26 4

The cover illustration shows the Bath mail coach
in early Victorian times

Produced through Print Production Services, Baughurst, Hants
Printed in Great Britain by J.W. Arrowsmith Ltd., Bristol

Contents

Acknowledgements

I would like to thank the staffs of Bath Reference Library, Wiltshire County Library, the Wiltshire Archaeological & Natural History Society's Library, the Wiltshire, Berkshire and Greater London Record Offices, and the Bruce Castle Postal Museum.

Mr Terry Crawford and Mr Harold Scott went to some trouble to provide information on cycle racing along the Bath Road, and Mr K. Gannon on Brunel's first visit to Reading. I am grateful to them, and also to the publishers, Mr and Mrs Nicholas Battle, who have been unfailingly helpful and encouraging ever since I suggested writing a book about the Great Bath Road.

Daphne Phillips

1

The Rise of Bath

This day from Salsb. I wrote by the post my excuse for not coming home which I hope will do for I am resolved to see the Bath ... Samuel Pepys, *Diary, 11 June 1668.*

On 11 June Pepys' leave of absence from the Navy Board was over. In the six days granted to him he and his companions had travelled in a hired coach to visit his father in Huntingdonshire, and then continued to Oxford, and south to Salisbury. There they had hired saddle horses and a guide and ridden 'over the plain and some prodigious great hills even to fright us' to see Stonehenge, which so impressed them that they declared it 'worth going this journey to see.'

Their summer tour was proving immensely enjoyable but, as is the way with holidays, too short. Forty miles to the north-west lay Bath, famous for the natural wonder of its hot mineral springs, and not far beyond that, the great port and city of Bristol. For a keen tourist and officer of the Navy Board such places were not to be missed. So, Pepys' letter of excuse despatched, they set out at six o'clock in the evening of 11 June for Bath, or the Bath, as it was often called in the 17th and 18th centuries. Somewhere along the way they took a wrong turning and found themselves, as night came on, at a little inn at Chitterne, where the landlord obligingly turned a pedlar out of a room to accommodate them. Not at all put out by their misadventure, the whole party was 'mighty merry at supper', and still merry next morning, in spite of waking to find themselves lousy. The pedlar had his revenge.

With the landlord to guide them (a service commonly provided by country innkeepers) the rest of the journey was accomplished safely, and they reached Bath before dark on 12 June. Pepys, eager to see the sights, walked out immediately with the landlord to look at the baths. 'They are not so large as I expected', he commented in his diary, 'but yet pleasant and the town most of stone and clean though the streets generally narrow. I home and being weary went to bed without supper.'

Next morning they were up at four o'clock, ready to be carried by sedan chair to the Cross Bath, where they hoped to enjoy the water before it became too crowded. Their hopes were disappointed. They had not been there long before a great many other people arrived, including some very fine ladies whom Pepys found pretty enough, 'only methinks it cannot be clean to go so many bodies together in to the same water.' Nevertheless, he remained in it for more than two hours, and was then wrapped in a sheet and carried back to the inn, where he went to bed and sweated for an hour. As he lay relaxing, a small band of musicians came to play to him, whom he judged as good as any he had heard in London.

At eleven o'clock that same morning they set out on a day trip to Bristol, where Pepys was keen to see the shipyards, the quay and the Custom House. They dined with friends and drove back by moonlight to Bath. The next day being Sunday, there was no travelling. They strolled around Bath, admiring the Abbey, the Market Place, the handsome stone houses, and the old city walls, then in a fair state of preservation. Pepys twice attended services in the Abbey, where he enjoyed the music but thought the preacher a 'vain Pragmatic fellow', and so slept through most of the evening sermon. On Monday, after a final look at the baths and reaching the satisfactory conclusion that the King's and Queen's Baths were 'full of a mixed sort of good and bad' and the Cross Bath only fit for gentry such as themselves, they settled their account at the inn (a total of £1.8s. 6d. plus 3 shillings for the servants) and set out on the journey back to London.

They had seen Bath; as much of it as there was then to see. The Roman city of Aquae Sulis, with its magnificent complex of baths and temple of Minerva, lay buried beneath the medieval streets, and was not to be discovered for more than 200 years. The Georgian city, with its elegant streets and crescents, its Pump Room and Assembly Rooms, was not yet even a dream. Bath was still a small provincial town, unique only in its possession of the hot springs which had led to the foundation of Aquae Sulis, and were again, in a new age of classicism, to bring it wealth and fame.

In the Middle Ages, baths had been built and administered by the abbey; the King's Bath for royal guests and other baths for the sick and poor. The wealth of the townspeople, however, had been derived mainly from the manufacture of woollen cloth. After the dissolution of the abbey, the baths came under the control of the city council, and as the cloth industry slowly but inexorably decayed, the city came to depend increasingly on the baths and the visitors who came there for health and pleasure. In the 16th century there was a growing interest in the curative properties of mineral springs. Learned physicians recommended them, and the public, appalled by the unpleasantness of most medical remedies, and the growing conviction that they were useless, turned hopefully towards this pleasant and painless form of treatment. The waters of Bath, unequalled anywhere in heat or volume, inspired a number of learned treatises; an early one by William Turner appearing in 1562. Ten years later, John Jones, 'Gent. and Graduate of Physicke', wrote another, claiming that the waters were 'wonderful and most excellent agaynst very many sicknesses, approved by authoritie, confirmed by reason, and dayly tried by experience.' These, and other encomiums, did much to attract increasing numbers of patients to Bath, so that the council soon found it necessary to appoint a Sergeant to supervise the baths and several assistants to attend to the bathers.

Encouragement came from Queen Elizabeth, who visited Bath in 1574, when she remarked upon the bad smells and the ruinous state of the church. Efforts were made to reduce the former and, under the Queen's sponsorship, funds were raised to begin the restoration of the latter. When next she came to Bath, in 1591, Elizabeth granted it a charter of self-government. Success brought its own problems. The city's reputation began to suffer from swarms of beggars who made themselves a nuisance to the authorities and to visitors; while the spectacle of nude mixed bathing, then the custom at Bath, attracted crowds of vulgar riff-raff and discouraged more desirable visitors. Henrietta Maria, the fastidious Queen of Charles I, refused to go there, but after the Restoration the broader-minded later Stuarts renewed royal patronage of Bath and helped to make it a pleasure resort for fashionable society. From that time, gambling became as great an attraction as bathing. Queen Anne, a lifelong invalid who suffered from gout, found the waters beneficial and visited Bath on several occasions. The court, the nobility and gentry, and crowds of hangers-on, were all happy to follow her there.

Towards the end of the 17th century, drinking the water began to be recommended as well as bathing, and in order to allow patients access to it directly from the spring, a pump was installed at the King's Bath. Another form of treatment then in vogue was pumping water onto afflicted parts of the body. In June 1676 Anthony Wood of Oxford went to Bath for the recovery of his hearing. He recorded that he received at the pump in the King's Bath over 9,200 pumps on his head, but went home at the end of a fortnight having found no remedy for his deafness.

When Celia Fiennes visited Bath in the 1680s she noted that changes were taking place. New houses, well furnished for visitors, had been built and other amenities improved. The ritual of bathing had been made more elaborate, and, as is made clear in her description of her own visit to the Cross Bath, very much more decent.

'The Cross in the middle has seates round it for the Gentlemen to sitt and round the walls are arches with seates for the Ladyes – all stone, and the seate is stone and if you think the seate is too low they raise it with a coushon as they call it, another Stone, but indeed the water bears you up that the seate seemes as easy as a down

8

The King's and Queen's Baths, about 1675. From a drawing by
Thomas Johnson

coushon; before the Arch the Ladyes use to have a laced
toilet hung up on top of the Arch, and so to shelter their
heads even to the water if they please; you generally sit up
to the neck in water; this Cross bath is much the coolest
and is used mostly in the heate of summer; there are
Galleries round the top that the Company that does not
bathe that day walkes in and lookes over into the bath on
their acquaintance and company. There are such a
number of Guides to each bath, of women to waite on the
ladyes and of men to waite on the gentlemen, and they
keep their due distance; there is a Serjeant belonging to
the baths that all the bathing tyme walkes in galleryes and
takes notice order is observed, and punishes the rude, and
most people of fashion sends to him when they begin to
bathe, then he takes particular care of them and
complements you every morning, which deserves its
reward at the end of the Season. When you walk about the
bath I use to have a woman guide or two to lead me, for

the water is so strong it will quickly tumble you down; and then you have 2 of the men guides goes at a distance about the bath to cleare the way; ... Ladyes goes into the bath with garments made of fine yellow canvas, which is stiff and made large with great sleeves like a parsons gown, the water fills it up so that its borne off that your shape is not seen, it does not cling as close as other linning which lookes sadly in the poorer sort that go in their own linning, the Gentlemen have drawers and wastcoates of the same sort of canvas, this is the best linning, for the bath water will change any other yellow.'

On leaving the water Celia ascended a flight of steps to a private room, where women guides removed her canvas dress, wrapped her in a flannel nightgown and put on her slippers. Like Pepys, she was then carried in a sedan chair, covered inside and out with red baize to make it warm and private, to her lodging, where she lay in bed and sweated, while her own maid and the maids of the house waited on her.

Apart from the taking the waters she found the amusements at Bath rather limited. 'The town with all its accommodations is adapted to the batheing and drinking of the waters, and to nothing else', but visitors could go for pleasant walks around the abbey or in the King's Mead, where there were 'little Cake-houses where you have fruit Sulibubs and sumer liquours.' The town could be hot and stuffy, but it was so surrounded by steep hills that few people cared to climb up to take the air. The food was good, with plenty of meat and fish, and prices were reasonable. 'The chargeableness of Bath is the lodgings and firing, the faggotts being very small but they give you very good attendance there.'

By the end of the 17th century a few other amenities had been provided. There were bowling greens and coffee houses to help while away the daylight hours, and evening entertainments in the new guildhall, a handsome building set on stone pillars and containing a spacious room for balls and card parties. According to Ned Ward, a visitor in 1700, the guildhall doorstep was guarded by 'a couple of Brawney Beadles to keep out the Mobility', but inside there was fine dancing, delicate music both vocal and instrumental, and a splendid collation of sweet-meats and wine.

About this time the city revived the legend of its foundation by King Bladud who, according to medieval chroniclers, was one of the early kings of Britain. In his youth Bladud had been stricken with leprosy, which forced him to leave the court and live a solitary life as a swineherd. Discovering by chance that a skin disease which afflicted his pigs was cured by wallowing in the steaming mud which then surrounded the hot springs, he followed their example, and he too was cured. On his return to the royal court, Bladud caused baths to be built over the springs so that other sufferers might benefit from the healing waters. Dr Pierce, a Bath physician, produced his own version of the tale in 1697. It was excellent publicity material, establishing the ancient fame of the waters even before the Romans came, and the council caused a statue of Bladud to be set in a niche overlooking the King's Bath.

In the 18th century Bath became England's leading health and pleasure resort, a place to which fashionable society could retreat in summer to recover from the fatigues and excesses, physical and financial, of the London season; and at the same time continue to enjoy each other's company in a round of social engagements. Formerly, the approach of summer had been the signal for the nobility and gentry to retire to their country estates, where the tedium of rural solitude might be enlivened only by the company of rustic squires and parsons. Bath offered a welcome alternative.

By that time many other spas were in existence. Springs all over the country had been discovered and promoted, but few resulted in spas much bigger than villages. Nearly all the springs were cold; some had offensive smells; some were in bleak or inaccessible places; none could compete in heat or volume with those at Bath. Even in the warm bath at Buxton, the water, according to Celia Fiennes, who tried them all, was 'not so warme as milke from the cow.' At Tunbridge, where a chalybeate spring had been discovered in 1606, an elegant and fashionable watering place grew up, although there too the water was cold and recommended mainly for drinking. Tunbridge Wells, however, was only a short journey from London, and this advantage, together with Queen Anne's liking for the place, and the part-time services of Beau Nash as Master of Ceremonies, made it, in the early 18th century at least, Bath's principal rival.

The amenities at Bath were very soon found to be inadequate for the increasing numbers of wealthy, leisured visitors, requiring not only accommodation and attendance at the baths, but more facilities for indoor and outdoor amusements, more high-class shops, coffee houses, musical and theatrical entertainments, and the services of a variety of trades and professions. When the 18th century opened, Bath had no concert hall, no theatre, and no place of public assembly other than the guildhall. Although drinking the water was becoming more popular, medically and socially, than bathing, people were obliged to drink it in the open air, whatever the weather.

Gradually, all these wants were supplied. In 1706 the first Pump Room was opened. There, visitors could drink the water in comfort, receiving their prescribed glasses from waiters in attendance at the pump and then strolling about the room, chatting to friends or listening to a small orchestra which played in the balcony overhead. In 1708 Thomas Harrison, a local developer, built the first assembly rooms, overlooking a popular place of promenade also laid out by him. There the Company (as visitors to Bath were collectively called) could meet to play cards, gossip, drink tea or chocolate and listen to music. Harrison's rooms were enlarged in 1720 by the addition of a ballroom. Reading was another favourite pastime, particularly with invalids, and in 1724 one of the first commercial lending libraries in the country was opened in Bath. Also during this period the council carried out improvements to the paving, lighting, cleaning and policing of the streets.

The social life of the resort was organised by a Master

Beau Nash, from the portrait by Thomas Hudson, in 1740

of Ceremonies, an office which Beau Nash raised to such importance that he has sometimes been seen as the principal creator of 18th century Bath. As a young man of no fixed profession save that of gamester, Nash arrived in Bath about 1705 and quickly recognised that here was a world of opportunity for someone endowed with his particular abilities, charm and persuasive powers. The reigning Master of Ceremonies was a certain Captain Webster, a gamester like himself, but one who devoted most of his time to drinking and gaming, and troubled himself with few events beyond a weekly ball in the guildhall. Very soon Nash was acting as his assistant, and when Webster was killed in a duel by a man who had lost heavily to him at cards, Nash stepped easily into his place.

According to Oliver Goldsmith in his biography of Beau Nash, the amusements of Bath at that time were 'neither elegant, nor conducted with delicacy. General society among people of rank or fortune was by no means established. The nobility still preserved a tincture of Gothic haughtiness, and refused to keep company with the gentry at any of the public entertainments of the place. Smoking in the Rooms was permitted; gentlemen and ladies appeared in a disrespectful manner at public entertainments in aprons and boots ... If the company liked each other, they danced till morning; if any person lost at cards, he insisted on continuing the game till luck should turn.'

The new Master of Ceremonies saw that his task was complex. Bath was sadly short of amenities, so that he must interest himself in every project for improvement. At the same time, the Company itself needed taking in hand. So large a gathering of strangers required someone to perform introductions and to help the nobility and gentry to mingle agreeably at public assemblies. The social rank of visitors was generally high in the early decades of the century, but country squires and city merchants were equally anxious to go there, and since entry to Bath society was not governed by such strict rules as applied in London there were occasions when the lower ranks provoked the Gothic haughtiness described by Goldsmith. Nash chose to regard all visitors on equal terms as his guests, and by laying down rules for the conduct of social events and publishing a code of manners which applied to everyone, he endeavoured to blend the various elements into one harmonious and truly polite society.

He disapproved strongly of informal dress at social functions, smoking in public rooms, disorganised gambling, dances which reeled on into the small hours, and above all of the customs of duelling and wearing swords. The rules he laid down were aimed at putting an end to such bad habits, and the methods he used for dealing with offenders were bold and effective. When the Duchess of Queensberry appeared at an assembly wearing a white lace apron (as was then the custom among ladies on informal occasions) the Beau stripped it from her, saying that only abigails wore aprons; and such was his standing that the Duchess took it in good part and even begged his pardon. Similarly, any gentlemen appearing in the Rooms in riding boots was likely to be asked if he had forgotten to bring his horse, so that very soon boots, like aprons, were seen no more at assemblies. When Princess Amelia, daughter of George II, asked for one more dance after the Beau had signalled the music to stop at the end of a ball, she was informed that the rules of Bath were unalterable. The Princess was not pleased but had to acquiesce. The wearing of swords Nash forbade absolutely, considering it a barbarous habit which encouraged duelling. Duels were still arranged, although discreetly; but if news of such an affair reached Nash he did his best, with the co-operation of the city authorities, to stop the meeting. It was not for nothing that the Master of Ceremonies was also known as the King of Bath.

So autocratic was his government of his small kingdom that he can only have reigned so long because society in general appreciated his high standards and the excellence of the entertainments provided at Bath. He commanded the respect, or at least the amused tolerance, of the highest in the land, from whom he received many gifts; and only a few people disliked him. Sarah, Duchess of Marlborough, and Alexander Pope, both as autocratic as he was, were among those who complained of his upstart impudence. It is possible that society amused itself by pretending to credit him with achievements which were in fact outside his control, and in this way some of the legends surrounding him may have been started. He was said to have caused the Pump Room to be built, the streets of Bath to be paved and lighted, the lodging houses improved, and unruly sedan chairmen brought under control by the issue of a limited number of licences. Another legend, which has grown up since his lifetime, claims that he ordered pumps to be erected at intervals all along the Road from London to Bath in order to lay the dust for wealthy travellers. There is no evidence that the Bath Road pumps, of which a few survive, were put up until many years after his death.

Nash's role was to encourage and promote new

amenities provided by those with the power and financial resources to do so, and there is no doubt that his support must have been invaluable. When the first Pump Room was opened, it was he who welcomed visitors and hired a small orchestra to play there. When Harrison's Assembly Rooms were opened, Nash helped to make them the social centre of Bath by arranging regular concerts throughout the season. His position made him an ideal fund-raiser. Soon after his arrival he helped to raise nearly £1,800 towards the cost of much-needed repairs to the approach roads to the city; and many years later he was one of the official collectors for a proposed hospital for deserving cases of the sick poor, who still arrived in Bath in great numbers. This project was supported by many distinguished people, including Dr William Oliver, originator of the famous biscuit, John Wood, the city's principal architect, who made a gift of his plans and services as director of works, and Ralph Allen, the wealthy businessman and quarry-owner, who gave all the necessary stone as well as generous sums of money. The hospital, later known as the Royal Mineral Water Hospital, was founded in 1738, and Nash was its Treasurer until his death in 1761.

He received no salary for his services as Master of Ceremonies. In an age when nearly everyone gambled, he made what was considered a respectable living from gaming and cards. His successes enabled him to live in a luxurious house and to travel, when he went to London or Tunbridge Wells, in a style as fine as a lord's. His coach was drawn by six perfectly matched greys, and his entourage included his own coachman, a postilion, two footmen riding behind the coach, a running footman, a gentleman out of livery and outriders with French horns. The Beau's years of affluence were brought to an end by new laws regulating gambling and making illegal certain games at which he was most adept. After 1745 his circumstances were severely reduced, so that he was no longer in a position to influence society, and his final years were passed in poverty and squalor. The city council had shown its gratitude to him as early as 1716, when he was made an Honorary Freeman of Bath. When he died, at the age of 87, the council granted £50 towards his funeral, and laid him to rest in the abbey.

Nash's prime had seen the beginnings of the transformation of Bath into one of the most beautiful cities of Europe. With the arrival, in 1727, of John Wood, an ambitious young architect with plans to turn the city into a new Rome, Bath's classical glories began to take shape. The council wisely rejected Wood's more grandiose schemes for public buildings but commissioned him to design much-needed houses for people of taste and fashion. Queen Square, Gay Street and the Circus set new high standards for town housing; while as a country retreat for Ralph Allen, Wood built the magnificent mansion of Prior Park on Combe Down. After Wood's death, he was succeeded as the city's leading architect by his son, whose most important work was the Royal Crescent, linked by Brock Street to the Circus.

In the later decades of the 18th century Bath reached its zenith. Further schemes were devised for the expansion of the city, whose streets and crescents had already begun

View of Bath in the 18th century

17

to adorn the hillsides to the north and west. Until 1774 the Avon hemmed in the city on its eastern side, but after Pulteney Bridge was opened the Bathwick estate was developed, and more smart new houses became available in Laura Place and Great Pulteney Street. In 1785 Thomas Baldwin, then City Architect, produced a plan for improving the old part of the town around the baths, transforming the medieval lanes into elegant streets linking the baths and the abbey with the newer part of the town, and making use of colonnades to shelter invalids on their way to the baths. By 1791 the Pump Room had become so inadequate that Baldwin designed the much larger Pump Room which survives today.

During the 18th century the timing and length of the Bath season changed considerably. Originally a short season of two or three months in summer, it became two seasons in spring and autumn which gradually expanded through the winter, so that by the 1760s the season lasted six full months. The growing popularity of spending the winter in Bath was due to the improvement of amenities and greater comforts provided in the lodging houses and public buildings. This trend continued, and by the 1780s the season extended from September to May, a full nine months.

There are no very reliable figures of the numbers of visitors to Bath but it was estimated that there were around 8000 each season at the beginning of the century, and 12000 by the 1740s. The *Bath Journal*, commencing publication in 1744, soon began to include regular lists of the most distinguished new arrivals. In 1746 these totalled 510; in 1760 2525; in 1780 3091; and in 1800 5341. The increases were partly due to paper's more diligent enquiries, and partly to the extension of the lists from the cream of the nobility to persons of lower rank. In the 1760s the visitors still included a high proportion of titled persons; in 1765, for instance, there were three princes, four dukes, a marquess, 24 earls with countesses, 14 viscounts, 43 viscountesses, 12 barons, an archbishop, and five bishops. The gentry made up the bulk of the visitors, but the wealthy merchant and manufacturing classes were well represented and their numbers increased as the century advanced.

Bath welcomed new arrivals with a peel of bells. Watchers on the approach roads swiftly relayed intelligence to the city concerning the identity and social standing of visitors, sometimes assessing their importance from the style of coach and the number of servants in attendance. Such information was of vital interest to lodging house keepers and tradesmen as well as to the city authorities. As soon as they were installed in their lodgings, visitors were serenaded by the city waits, a pleasure for which a nobleman was charged half a guinea and a commoner five shillings. The expenses of a visit to Bath soon began to mount up, for the bellringers also expected a fee of a guinea or half a guinea; and then there was the subscription of two guineas to the Assembly Rooms, and a guinea to join a library, where newspapers could be read, books borrowed, and, for an extra charge, pens and paper obtained for writing letters.

Bath's reputation as a pleasure resort far outshone its reputation as a health resort, although people continued to go there for both reasons and the welfare of patients was always a primary concern of the city council. Contemporary letters, newspapers and memoirs contain many references to sad and painful journeys undertaken by the sick and dying; and the walls of Bath Abbey are lined with monuments to wealthy and distinguished people who came from all over Britain and distant parts of the empire to spend their last days in Bath. The names and deeds of most of these are now forgotten. It is as a pleasure resort that Bath lives on, in the novels, plays and letters of the great writers of the age; and no city outside London can boast so long and glittering a list of famous visitors from the world of literature, art and the theatre. Among them were Alexander Pope, Henry Fielding, Samuel Richardson, Oliver Goldsmith, Samuel Johnson, Tobias Smollett, Jane Austen, Fanny Burney, Thomas Gainsborough, William Hoare, Thomas Lawrence, James Quin, David Garrick, Sarah Siddons and Richard Brinsley Sheridan.

Pump Room scene, from *The Comforts of Bath*, by Thomas
Rowlandson, 1798

Towards the end of the 18th century Bath lost its
fashionable and exclusive character, but it remained
extremely popular. Large numbers of lesser gentry and
city merchants continued to go there with their wives and
families. They could spend their money, enjoy the
excellent amenities, and mingle with the wealthy
dowagers, elderly generals and sea captains, and retired
professional men who, by that time, formed the majority
of Bath's permanent residents.

2

The Route of the Bath Road

So out and lost our way which made me vexed but came into
it again. And in the evening betimes came to Reading.
Samuel Pepys, *Diary, 16 June 1668.*

The road which became famous as the Great Bath Road
was not an ancient or even a medieval road, but an 18th
century development designed to serve the ever-growing
numbers of travellers to the premier spa at Bath. During
the Roman occupation, London had been linked with
Bath by a road running via Silchester, Speen, Mildenhall
and Sandy Lane, but this route was abandoned as later
roads came into existence, serving different destinations.
A highway grew up between London and Bristol; and the
proximity of Bath to Bristol was to be an important factor
in the later development of the Bath Road.

The route from London to the two towns was the same
as far as Marlborough, but from there, and from
Beckhampton and Chippenham, three roads turned off
towards Bath. Those from Marlborough and
Beckhampton went over the Downs by way of
Shepherd's Shore, Beacon Hill, Sandy Lane and Bowden
Hill to Lacock. From Lacock a medieval road twisted
through the villages of Gastard and Neston to Kingsdown
and Bath, but by the 17th century the more usual route
was from Lacock to Corsham, and thence to Chapel
Plaister, Kingsdown and Bath.

Although the six main post roads radiating from
London, of which the Bristol road was one, were laid

The old road still clearly visible as it descends Beacon Hill near Heddington and proceeds past the camera to Sandy Lane

down in the 17th century, roads at that time were not clearly defined. In many places they divided into more than one track, so that travellers could choose which way to go according to the weather and the state of the road surface. Usually they had a choice between high and low ground, so that when a valley road was flooded or too deep in mud they could take to the hillsides until the lower road was again viable. On the Bath and Bristol road, for instance, the more direct route crossed the marshy area around Hungerford and continued through Froxfield and Savernake; but a heavily used alternative route avoided Hungerford and ran along the lower slopes of the hills north of the Kennet through Ramsbury to

22

Marlborough. Similarly, beyond Marlborough, an ancient road struck out over Manton Down and swung to the south-west past Avebury and Beckhampton to continue over the Downs by way of Shepherd's Shore. Pepys drove along this road on his return journey from Bath in 1668, reflecting that a shepherd's life could only be pleasant in fair weather, and marvelling at the great sarsens covering the ground between Avebury and Marlborough.

Finding the way from place to place in the 17th century was not easy. Pepys, in the quotation at the beginning of this chapter, records that they lost their way between Newbury and Reading, two towns which are today joined by a road on which it would be very difficult to lose the way. It is interesting to speculate on where they went wrong. Did they take the road northwards from Newbury towards Shaw and miss the turning to Thatcham? Or did they wander into the maze of lanes crossing Bucklebury

A stage wagon climbing a hilly road in the 17th century

23

Common? We shall never know. Like most well-to-do travellers, Pepys often hired a guide through unfamiliar country, but on this route he evidently expected his coachman to manage without one. When they left Bath on the previous day they had been a little afraid of losing the way as they drove over the Downs, but they had reached Marlborough safely and passed a comfortable night at the White Hart. On the second day of their three-day journey to London, they had found the way apparently without difficulty through Ramsbury and Chilton Foliat to Newbury, where they stopped to dine before going on to Reading. It was then that they went astray. Perhaps they were all feeling rather drowsy after dinner, and were less vigilant than they had been earlier in the day. Perhaps the trouble was that roads then looked very much alike; widths and standards of repair varied on all roads, and signposting hardly existed. Even had the travellers known where they were, they could not have put themselves on the right road by consulting a map, for no road maps were yet available. Travellers without guides had to depend on information supplied by innkeepers, fellow travellers and local inhabitants.

The earliest map of the roads to Bath and Bristol appeared in John Ogilby's *Britannia*, an atlas of the principal roads of Britain published in 1675. Ogilby employed a team of surveyors to measure and collect information on all the principal roads from London, and all the most important cross-roads connecting provincial towns. Each road was drawn out in strips, showing the places through which it passed, the destinations of the side turnings, the mileage, hills, rivers, bridges, woods and other features as they occurred along the way. So long as a traveller kept to the road described, the map was invaluable; once he strayed from it he was lost in uncharted country.

In Ogilby's time there was no road called the Bath Road. The road from London to the city of Bristol was one of the principal roads in his atlas, and the three turnings to Bath were indicated along this road. The route was as follows.

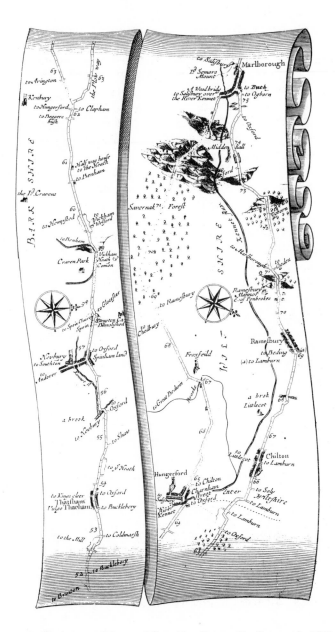

Ogilby's map of the road from Reading to Marlborough, 1675

From London it ran through Knightsbridge and the villages of Kensington, Hammersmith and Turnham Green to the little town of Brentford, then to Hounslow. There the Bristol road parted company with the road to Staines and Lands End, and proceeded across three miles of heath to Longford, Colnbrook, 'Slow', and Maidenhead. There is crossed the Thames by a wooden bridge and passed through the town and Maidenhead Thicket to Hare Hatch, Twyford and Reading, where it crossed the Kennet and ran along the northern side of the valley to Theale, Woolhampton and Thatcham. Soon afterwards it crossed the Lambourn stream and ran quite close to the Kennet for half a mile before entering the northern part of Newbury known as Speenhamland.

Skirting Craven (now Benham) Park, it continued along the same route as the modern A4 to within a mile of the turning to Avington, where it divided into two alternative routes. One, which Ogilby called the Plow Way, turned to the north-west along Radley Bottom (it appears on modern maps as a track surviving only part of the way), and continued westwards in a fairly straight line through Leverton to Chilton Foliat. Keeping to the north of the Kennet it passed round Ramsbury manor, as the road does today, and ran along White Hill and across the road leading to Axford into a track shown on modern maps as Sound Bottom, from which it descended to the valley at Mildenhall and entered the town of Marlborough. Although this hilly route was reckoned by Ogilby to be nearly two miles longer than the alternative road through Hungerford, Froxfield and Savernake, it was clearly very much needed. At Hungerford, where the Dun joins the Kennet, the two streams provided valuable water meadows and fisheries, but they also created a wide marshy area which travellers did well to avoid in wet weather. And, although a bridge had existed at Hungerford at a much earlier date, it was perhaps not very stable, for Ogilby shows the road here plunging through a ford. Beyond Hungerford the land was still low-lying, while through the Forest of Savernake the trees crowded close beside the road, preventing the wind and sun from drying it, so that the mud was always deep.

Just before entering Marlborough Ogilby indicated the first turning to Bath, over Manton Down. The Bristol Road continued to Beckhampton, where a turning to the south-west was marked 'to Bathe by Sandy Lane'. The Bristol Road carried on over the top of Cherhill Hill into Calne, and down Derry Hill into Chippenham, where Ogilby marked the third turning to Bath before continuing along the main highway to Bristol. This third road to Bath was drawn in detail in another map in his atlas, showing the cross-road from Chippenham to Bath and Wells. It ran through Pickwick and Chapel Plaister to link up with the Beckhampton — Sandy Lane route into Bath by way of Kingsdown.

There were several notable differences between Ogilby's road to Bath and Bristol and the route followed today by the A4 and A420 to these cities. At the London end, the 17th century road ran along today's Kensington Road, Hammersmith Road, Chiswick High Road, Brentford High Street and Hounslow High Street; whereas the A4 runs along the Great West Road, which was built in the 1920s and 30s to bypass congested areas of west London. Further west along the A4 are other bypasses, made to speed traffic past villages which once flourished on the trade brought to them by the Bath Road: Longford, Colnbrook, Twyford and Theale. New roads have also diverted traffic round Maidenhead, Reading and Newbury.

The modern road runs through Chippenham to Corsham, and from there through Box along a road which was not built until the middle of the 18th century. The opening of this new road made the Chippenham route a much better one for coaches than the older one via Shepherd's Shore and Sandy Lane, so that after 1755 the latter was no longer maintained. It was still used by a few travellers, mostly horsemen, but the hillier sections soon fell into too bad a state for wheeled vehicles. The Old Bath Road, as it came to be known, can still be traced, winding from Lacock over Bowden Hill to Sandy Lane, and thence across the B3102 towards Heddington. A

The roads to Bath in the 1780s, showing the Old Bath Road and the roads via Calne and Devizes before alterations were made to these to bypass Cherhill Hill and Shepherd's Shore

28

Yatesbury
Field
Mill Hill
Barrows
Avebury
Roll Ditch
Cherhill Hill
Old Monastery
Ray
Down
Cangborough Hill
Long Stone
Old Down
Fore
Down
Overton
Down
Oldbury Castle
and Hill
Beckhampton Inn
Silbury
Hill
Beckhampton
Swallow
Head of Spring
West
Kennet
Beckhampton
Field
East Kennet
S   H   I   R   E
pherds
West Kennet
Field
Pound Down
Roughbridge Hill
Easton
Hill
St Anne Hill
Wansdyke
St Anns
Barn
Easton Spring
Easton
Milk Hill
Sommer
Down
the King
Hill
Burton Gr.
Black Burrin
annings
Upper Mill
South Horton
Clifford Hills
Walker
Hill
Farewell
White Leaze
Com.
Allington
Alton Priory
Lo Horton
Alton
Barns
Stanton
Barnard
Burbach Hill
Low Mill
Allcannings
Allcannings Farm
Woodborough
Hill
ale

short distance from the crossroads, on the left, are two old houses which used to be inns. One is a fine brick house which formerly was the Bear, where Queen Anne and other notable travellers broke their journeys. The other, now called Bell Farm, was the Bell Inn, a humbler establishment where coachmen and servants were accommodated. The road continues past Turnpike Farm until it becomes a wide, grassy, and increasingly rutted track climbing Beacon Hill to cross the Downs. Here and there, half hidden in the bushes at the side of the road, and its lettering long since worn away, an 18th century milestone survives as a clue to the former importance of this road.

The Chippenham route did not remain unrivalled for long. In the second half of the 18th century a low-level route through Devizes and Melksham to Bath was developed, and towards the end of the coaching era twice as many coaches were using this as were using the Chippenham route. At first the Devizes route went via Atworth, Blue Vein and Kingsdown, but about 1828 a road was cut through east of Blue Vein to Box village, avoiding Kingsdown Hill.

3

The Bath Road Turnpiked

From Redding to Theale sad clay deep way; thence to
Newbury all clay mirey ground.
Celia Fiennes, *Journeys, c. 1690.*

To the 20th century traveller, accustomed to signs
warning him of every conceivable hazard, 'Mud on the
road' rarely signifies more than a short distance of thinly
smeared road surface. For the 17th century traveller mud,
of a depth and extent undreamed of today, was the
commonest impediment to progress along the roads.
Mud was not merely spread over the surface; in places the
road was largely composed of mud, into which feet and
hoofs sank at every step, and the wheels of heavy wagons
and coaches dug ruts, sometimes axle deep, in which foul
water collected. Heavy clay soils were the most
troublesome, easily thwarting the efforts of the inexpert
roadmenders of the time to fill in the ruts and holes with
stones, flints, gravel, chalk or any rubbish which lay to
hand. The muddy miles along which Celia Fiennes rode
from Reading to Newbury ran along the Kennet valley,
and in her opinion compared very unfavourably with the
road to Newbury from the north, of which she wrote,
'Most of this way is much on the Downs and good roads.'

Complaints from many travellers of that time bear
eloquent witness to the state of the roads, but nothing was
done to improve them, and people continued to endure
endless delays and hardships, while men of business
urged that neither trade nor industry could expand so
long as the roads hindered the transport of goods. The
few public coach services which had been started in the

1640s and 50s were unable to run to any kind of timetable, even in the summer months, and in winter it was impossible for them to run at all. Difficulties of communication effectively isolated towns and villages from one another, so that each community had to be as self-sufficient as possible. Villages looked upon the nearest market town as the centre of social, economic and administrative affairs, and many people never ventured further than that from home throughout their lives.

These small communities, with their limited horizons, were responsible for the upkeep of the roads. An act for mending the highways, passed in 1555, required the inhabitants of each parish to choose annually one of their number to be surveyor of the highways, with power to call upon the rest of them to work for four (later six) consecutive days a year at mending the roads. All labour, tools, carts and teams of horses had to be provided freely by the inhabitants, and they were bound to be ready on the appointed days to work under the surveyor's direction for eight hours each day. Defaulters could be fined, and it was one of the surveyor's more disagreeable duties to report them to the local Justice of the Peace, to whom he himself was answerable. This act remained the basis of highway administration for nearly 300 years. The turnpike system which developed in the 18th century did not make statute labour unnecessary but, on the contrary, often made use of it; and, in any case, all unturnpiked roads remained the responsibility of the parishes.

Statute labour was very unpopular. The loss of six days' wages, or of the use of horses and carts for the sake of mending the roads, caused resentment and hardship. People who could afford to pay fines often preferred to do so, while others sent unwilling substitutes. In the 16th century William Harrison complained that 'the rich do so cancel their portions and the poor so loiter in their labours, that of all the six, scarcely two good days' work are performed.' Pepys recorded on more than one occasion that he gave money 'to the poor and menders of the highway'; a fair indication of the level to which parish interest in road maintenance had sunk.

Stonebreakers working on a road, early 19th century

Lack of knowledge of sound road building methods lay at the root of the problem. The surveyor, in spite of his title, had no special knowledge or training. Usually he was a farmer or innkeeper, or some other practical man deemed capable of the task. Clearing ditches, draining water out of ruts and holes, filling these with stones and raking muddy gravel over the top was generally the extent of his skill. The weather and passing traffic soon undid the work, so that the task seemed hopeless. Many an incurable quagmire must have resembled Bunyan's Slough of Despond, into which cartloads of stones had sunk to no effect.

The parishes hardest hit by the system were those crossed by main highways used by long-distance travellers between London and major provincial towns. The incessant labour and expense of trying to maintain these roads became an intolerably heavy burden; and the only way of alleviating it was to make the travellers contribute towards the cost of mending the road. In 1663 the Justices of three counties crossed by the Great North Road obtained an Act of Parliament enabling them to erect three turnpike gates across the road, but they met with furious opposition. One gate was never erected; one was so easily evaded that it was useless; only at the third gate were tolls successfully collected. More than 30 years passed before the idea was adopted elsewhere. By the beginning of the 18th century the roads had deteriorated so badly that the turnpike system was revived in earnest, and a number of acts were passed placing particularly difficult stretches of highway under the control of local Justices of the Peace.

One of the first concerned the roads around Bath itself. The city lay low in a valley, surrounded by high hills, and all the roads leading into it were steep and rocky. An act for repairing them was obtained in the Parliamentary session of 1706-7. It claimed that Bath was 'a place of very great resort from all parts of the Kingdom of Great Britain and from foreign parts, for the use and benefit of the baths, and drinking the mineral waters there', and that all the ancient roads for coaches, carts, wagons and other carriages, by reason of the great and heavy loads of goods and other things which were drawn through them, relating to the trade of Bristol and other nearby towns, as well as to the trade of Bath, had become very ruinous and dangerous. The most important road listed in the act was the one leading through Batheaston to the top of Kingsdown Hill, five miles in length. This was the main road from London into Bath. All the roads were to be controlled by a committee of Justices representing the city of Bath and the counties of Wiltshire, Somerset and Gloucester, which was to meet at Bath Guildhall. Turnpike gates and toll-houses were to be set up on all the roads, and the tolls to be charged were a shilling for a coach or other vehicle drawn by more than two horses, sixpence for one drawn by one or two horses, a penny for a horse, tenpence for every score of oxen or cattle, and fivepence for every score of sheep or lambs. An interesting exception was made in the case of people going up onto the hills to take the air, a necessary exercise in a town which could be as hot and stuffy as Bath. These people, many of whom were visitors, were to pay the usual toll on going out, but could get their money back from the turnpike keeper who received it on their return to the town.

According to Defoe, it was on Kingsdown Hill that Queen Anne herself nearly suffered a serious accident when her coach began to roll backwards down the hill, and it was by her direction that the road began to be repaired. 'On the N.W. of this city', he wrote, 'up a very steep hill, is the King's Down, where sometimes persons of quality who have coaches go up for air ... And the hill up to the Downs is so steep, that the late Queen Anne was extremely frighted in going up, her coachman stopping to give the horses breath, and the coach wanting a dragstaff, run back in spite of all the coachman's skill; the horses not being brought to strain the harness again, or pull together for a good while, and the coach putting the guards behind it into the utmost confusion, till some of the servants setting their heads and shoulders to the wheels, stopped them by plain force.'

In the same year, 1706–7, the town of Calne obtained an act enabling it to turnpike three miles of road running through the town from Cherhill Hill to Studley Bridge. On both sides of the town the road crossed marshy river valleys. Calne, like many other west country towns, was a centre for the woollen industry, and the loads of woollen cloth, together with all the other goods and droves of animals passing through, inflicted heavy damage on a road always inclined to be wet and muddy. The act described the road as 'the ancient and direct highway and post road from the City of London to the severall citys of Bath and Bristol and the Southern parts of Wales', and claimed that it had become 'very ruinous and dangerous to all Her Majesty's subjects.'

The Calne road, too, was administered by local justices. But by the time the next act relating to the Bath Road was passed, a new kind of highway authority had evolved – the turnpike trust. This consisted of a number of local gentlemen – landowners, merchants and professional men, but not necessarily justices – who were empowered by an act of Parliament to erect turnpikes and to carry out such works as were necessary to put a particular length of road into good repair. In every case the initiative came from local people, who formed themselves into a committee, subscribed to the legal expenses, petitioned Parliament, and having obtained their act, became trustees.

Under the circumstances it was inevitable that road improvements would be patchy. Only a few miles of road were adopted by each trust, and these were usually disconnected, so that the turnpiking of the whole length of a major highway took several decades to complete. The system dictated that the worst stretches of road were repaired first; the nature of the soil, the steepness of gradients and the volume of traffic being decisive factors. Long-distance road improvement was further delayed because turnpiking was, at first, regarded as a temporary measure. Trusts were set up initially for a period of 21 years or less, in the rather naive belief that, once the road had been properly repaired, full responsibility for it could be handed back to the parish. Disillusionment very soon set in. By the time the later trusts were formed, all the earlier ones had been obliged to obtain acts renewing their powers, on the plea that the work had proved far more difficult and expensive than had been anticipated.

The turnpiking of the Bath Road took 50 years to complete, so that it was not until the second half of the 18th century that it was sufficiently improved to allow the greater speed and efficiency of travel which marked the finest years of the coaching age.

Since the Old Bath Road, from Beckhampton via Shepherd's Shore, Sandy Lane and Kingsdown to Bath, was the road the early coaches used, this was turnpiked first. The western end of it had been repaired under the Bath roads act of 1706-7. The eastern end, from Shepherd's Shore and over the Downs and the rugged slopes of Beacon Hill to a place called Horsley Upright Gate near Sandy Lane, was turnpiked in 1713. The central section, from Sandy Lane over Bowden Hill, and winding through Lacock, Corsham and Chapel Plaister to Kingsdown, was turnpiked in 1725.

The road from London to Bath via Chippenham took longer to complete, and the disjointed pattern of improvement can be seen in the following list, arranged topographically, of the different sections turnpiked and the dates when the acts were obtained.

Kensington to Cranford Bridge	1717
Cranford Bridge to Maidenhead Bridge	1727
Maidenhead Bridge to Twyford	1718
Twyford to Reading	1736
Reading to Puntfield (near Theale)	1714
Puntfield to Speenhamland (Newbury)	1728
Speenhamland to Marlborough	1726
Marlborough to Cherhill	1743
Cherhill to Studley Bridge	1707
Studley Bridge to Chippenham	1727
Chippenham to Corsham	1743
Corsham to Bath via Box	1756

Seven years after the town of Calne had turnpiked the road running through it, Reading followed suit by obtaining, in 1714, an act for repairing the Bath road on the western side of the town as far as Theale, the road described by Celia Fiennes as a 'sad clay deep way'. Very similar reasons were put forward to those at Calne. Numerous heavy loads of goods passing that way every day had made the road so very bad that it was dangerous to all persons, horses and cattle, and was almost impassable for six months every year. The goods traffic here included huge loads of malt, corn and timber on their way to the town wharves for shipment down the Thames to London. It was about this time that the first moves were being made to make the River Kennet navigable between Reading and Newbury, and when this was accomplished some of the heavy goods traffic was removed from the Bath Road.

The Reading to Puntfield Trust was originally set up for a period of only 15 years, but as this term drew to a close the trustees had to obtain a renewal act, on the grounds that, although large sums of money had been spent on the road, and great progress had been made in repairing it, the increasing traffic and the difficulty of fetching repair materials from a distance had caused the expense to be more than anticipated. The trust was renewed in 1728 for 21 years, and at the same time was empowered to take over a further eight miles between Theale and Newbury.

On the eastern side of Reading the road to London was not turnpiked until many years later, the delay being due partly to higher ground level and partly to motives protecting the town's trade. Not only was the long-established barge traffic to London so profitable as to make competition from an improved road undesirable, but Reading's important cattle market was held on the eastern side of the town, and there was strong opposition to the setting up of toll gates on any of the approach roads to the market. The Maidenhead to Twyford Trust, set up in 1718, was willing to take over the extra four miles from Twyford to Reading, and calculated that part of the income from its existing gates could be used to pay for the additional length of road. Not everyone agreed with this, and a petition was presented in the House of Commons pleading that the income would not be sufficient unless one of the gates was moved. The tolls currently produced about £585 a year, and expenses amounted to £255, so that only £330 was available for repairing the 16 miles of road from Maidenhead to Twyford. Moreover, the road had been so very badly damaged by severe winter weather that more money would be needed to put it into good repair. Unless the Twyford gate was moved nearer to Reading, the inhabitants of Sonning would not be made to contribute towards the upkeep of their main road into the town. Also, in summertime, thousands of sheep and cattle would continue to pass into Reading without paying toll. This petition was not successful. When in 1736 the Maidenhead Trust was empowered to take over the additional road, a clause in their act prohibited the erection of a gate 'between the Gallows and the end of

Ort Lane next the town of Reading', which effectively kept free several ways into the cattle market. The Twyford gate was not moved.

Turnpikes were never popular, and every proposed new trust met with opposition. When a bill was presented in Parliament for turnpiking the exceptionally busy road leading out of London through Kensington and Hounslow, petitions against it were received from a variety of sources, including carriers, drovers, stage-coach proprietors, merchants, landowners and farmers. They claimed that those responsible for the road had deliberately allowed it to fall into disrepair so that a turnpike could be set up and the expense of maintenance transferred to the road users. It was also alleged that only a small part of the proposed new turnpike road was really in need of repair. Evidently people had been accustomed to bad roads for so long that they were prepared to put up with anything rather than help to pay for better ones. A trust, however, was set up in 1717, and the twelve miles of road from Kensington to Cranford Bridge were turnpiked.

In rural west Berkshire and Wiltshire improvements came later than around the towns. The road from

The road down Marlborough hill in the 18th century

Newbury to Marlborough, passing through Hungerford and Savernake, was said to be so dreadfully muddy that it was almost impassable in spring and autumn as well as in winter, and so narrow in places that coaches and carriages could not pass each other. An act for repairing and widening this road came into force in 1726, but little seems to have been done to improve it until a renewal act was obtained in 1744. Until then the alternative route, known as the Ramsbury Narrow Way, continued to be well-used.

West of Marlborough the road to Beckhampton, together with the two branches to Cherhill on the Chippenham road, and to Shepherd's Shore on the Sandy Lane road, were turnpiked in 1743. In the following year the Chippenham Trust, which already maintained the road between that town and Calne, as far as Studley Bridge, obtained an act enabling it to take over a continuation of the Bath Road to Pickwick, in Corsham. This resulted in a much improved route for coaches through Chippenham for Bath, and, as the promoters of the new road had hoped, drew a number of regular stage-coaches as well as private carriages away from the Sandy Lane route. Travellers could now avoid both Beacon and Bowden Hills, although they had still to complete the journey into Bath by way of Chapel Plaister and Kingsdown Hill.

After 1745 the Sandy Lane route was used less and less, and the final blow for the trusts maintaining it came in 1756, when an act was passed for making an entirely new and slightly shorter road into Bath from the Cross Keys at Pickwick through Box and Batheaston, avoiding Kingsdown altogether. Four years later, in December 1761, the *Bath Journal* announced that 'The New Turnpike Road leading from Bath through Box to Chippenham, Calne and Marlborough is now completed and opened, reducing the distance by 1½ miles.' Essentially, this completed the line of the Great Bath Road.

4

The Turnpike Trusts at Work

This custom prevailing, 'tis more than probable, that our
posterity may see the roads all over England restored in time
to such perfection, that travelling and carriage of goods will
be much more easy both to man and horse, than ever it was
since the Romans lost this island.
Daniel Defoe, *A Tour through the Whole Island of Great Britain,*
1724-6.

Turnpike trustees held their meetings at principal local
inns, sometimes using two or three at different places on
their road in rotation, sometimes a variety of inns in the
town in which they were based. The Reading to
Speenhamland Trust met at the Mitre in Reading and the
Globe in Newbury, but occasionally used other inns. The
Colnbrook Trust often met at the George in Colnbrook
and the Windmill or the Castle at Salt Hill, but it also met
at the Angel, the Swan and the Ostrich in Colnbrook, and
at the Crown and the Bear in Slough. The Maidenhead to
Reading Trust met fairly regularly at the Bear in
Maidenhead and the Crown in Reading, and in later years
at Maidenhead Town Hall. Calne Trust met at the
Lansdowne Arms and the White Hart; Chippenham
Trust at the Angel or the Town Hall.

Each turnpike act contained a list of names of those
who were to serve as trustees, and these usually included
the local nobility and gentry, who were the largest
landowners, mayors and aldermen of boroughs, and a
variety of professional men, such as solicitors, doctors,
clergymen, and retired army and navy officers. In some
acts the list of trustees ran to over a hundred, but most of

these were included merely to show the strength of local support for the turnpike. Minutes of trust meetings show that very few trustees attended or took any active part in the trust's affairs. Only a very small number, between five and nine, were needed for a quorum, and all too often less than that turned up, and the meeting was adjourned. The clerk then had to arrange for notices of a revised date to be displayed at the turnpike gates, and wait for the next meeting.

Some show of enthusiasm was seen at the first few meetings, when such vital matters as the appointment of officers, the line of the road and the position of gates were decided. The officers included a treasurer, a clerk, one or more surveyors, and gatekeepers. The treasurer and clerk were sometimes salaried but only part-time officers. The surveyor, who did the lion's share of the work, was full-time and received a salary of about £20 a year. Gatekeepers were paid up to ten shillings a week. The Colnbrook Trust, set up in 1727 to repair the road from Cranford Bridge to the Buckinghamshire end of Maidenhead Bridge, gave one of their surveyors the job of ticketter, responsible for numbering and stamping the turnpike tickets and delivering them to the gatekeepers, from whom he collected the toll money.

The treasurer was an important and influential officer, responsible for receiving and holding funds, making disbursements and keeping the trust's accounts. It was usual for the trustees to choose one of themselves for this office, and incumbent on them to choose a man of sound repute, whose good name would encourage people to invest in the trust, for loans were essential. Although most trust income was derived from tolls, the trustees were nearly always obliged to mortgage these in order to cover the legal costs of obtaining their Act of Parliament and to pay for initial road improvements. Unlike canal or railway enterprises, turnpike trusts were created to maintain existing facilities, not to construct new ones, and they were therefore not permitted to raise capital by the issue of shares. In addition to first loans, trusts invariably found, as the work of improving the road proceeded, that further loans were needed for a number of purposes, such as major road widening and straightening schemes, building more substantial toll houses, or obtaining renewal acts. As their number grew, and they became established on a long-term basis throughout the country, turnpike trusts became an important sector for local investment.

The clerk was often a local solicitor. Apart from legal matters, his duties included handling correspondence, placing advertisements in the press, and taking the minutes at meetings. Not all trusts kept minutes of their early meetings, and some did not do so until the General Turnpike Act of 1773 made this compulsory. On the Bath Road, the Colnbrook Trust was one of the few which kept minutes from the beginning, and some of these have survived. They show the trust taking initial steps to make their stretch of road wider and safer. The clerk is instructed to give notice in writing to land owners that trees or other obstructions beside the road must be removed; and to bridge owners that necessary repairs must be carried out before a certain date. In default, the trustees could cause the work to be done forthwith. Turnpike trusts were powerful bodies, and meant business.

The surveyor was the busiest and most important of the trust's officers. His essential duty was to supervise the repair of the road under the direction of the trustees, and this involved a variety of tasks. He had to make detailed reports to the trustees on the state of the road, and of any watercourses affecting it; notify them of obstructions which ought to be cleared away, and places where extra land was needed for widening; and make contact with the private or corporate owners of bridges in need of strengthening or rebuilding. He was also responsible for obtaining supplies of gravel, chalk, stones and other repair materials. Early turnpike acts authorised surveyors to take these freely from any waste or common land, and from private land on payment only for damage done, but later it became usual to negotiate a reasonable price for materials with the owner of the land.

The Bath Road from Brentford to Colnbrook, about 1790

Above all, the surveyor had to deal with the thorny problem of getting a sufficient labour force to carry out the necessary work. Turnpike trusts were set up to raise additional revenues and to reinforce highway law with respect to a particular stretch of road, not to relieve the parishes of their duty of repairing it, and every trust was entitled to a proportion of statute labour from each parish. This was not given willingly; the parishes, after all, were still responsible for maintaining all the other roads

within their boundaries. A year after the Colnbrook Trust was set up, their surveyor was ordered to measure the length of road passing through each parish, so that application could be made to the county Justices in Quarter Sessions to determine what proportion of their six days annual labour the inhabitants should give to the turnpike road. In 1729, the Justices for Middlesex decided on the following: Harlington 3 days; Harmondsworth 3 days; Cranford 2 days; Bedfont 1 day; Hanwell 1 day. Most early trusts followed a similar procedure, endeavouring to obtain at least some free labour before hiring whatever additional labour was needed on the open market. An assortment of paid and unpaid workmen can never have been satisfactory, and many trusts found that trying to exact statute labour was hardly worth the trouble. Two months after the decision of the Middlesex Justices, the Colnbrook Trustees ordered their surveyor to present a bill of indictment at the next Quarter Sessions against the inhabitants of Cranford for not performing their statute labour. In the Buckinghamshire section of their road, the inhabitants of Taplow were equally uncooperative, and the Colnbrook Trust brought a similar bill against them.

Turnpike acts soon began to empower trusts to compound with parishes for an annual sum of money in lieu of statute labour. This sum was raised by a parish rate. The Maidenhead Trust began its second term in 1728 with an act which made no reference to statute labour, and allowed the trustees to compound for whatever sum they thought reasonable. The Reading Trust, when taking over extra mileage of road from Puntfield to Speenhamland in 1728, was granted powers to exact statute labour or to compound. But in Wiltshire a rather more feudal attitude prevailed. The trust set up in 1726 to repair the road from Speenhamland through Savernake Forest to Marlborough included two Earls, a Baron, a Viscount, and four Baronets among its leading trustees, and the wording of their act made it clear that they intended to stand no nonsense from the peasantry. All persons who by law were chargeable towards repairing the roads should remain chargeable and do their respective works as before they ought to have done, it said, and there was no mention of compounding. When this trust was renewed in 1744, another clause was inserted saying that parish surveyors must bring lists of names of persons obliged to do statute work and that the trustees would allot work as they thought fit. Each team of men and horses was to work three days a year, and the fines imposed for each day of absence were three shillings for each horse and one shilling and sixpence for each labourer.

Further evidence of the tough attitude taken by this trust can be seen in their decision to appoint persons to find out whether any of the money collected at the gates was being misapplied, or whether there were any abuses of power or authority. Moreover, while the newly made road was draining and settling, the surveyor was authorised to put up fences or bars across it at every mile, so that coaches and carriages, foot passengers and droves of cattle must 'go in the Old Tracks during that time.' Notices warning travellers of this were to be put up at turnpike gates and other public places; and there was, of course, a fine of ten shillings for anyone who pulled down any of the bars or fences. Under the circumstances it was hardly surprising that at least one elderly Marlborough coachman refused to use the new road at all and, according to a story in the *Gentleman's Magazine* in 1752, persisted in going round by the Ramsbury narrow way. One by one he lost all his passengers, and when asked why he was so obstinate in refusing to use the better road, he said that he was now an aged man, and that his grandfather and father had driven along the old road before him, and he would continue to do so until he died, even though his four horses drew only a passenger fly.

Toll gates were set up as soon as each trust went into action, and often consisted of a temporary barrier until a proper gate had been made and erected. The gatekeeper, too, might have to put up with a makeshift shelter until his cottage was built. In view of the fact that turnpike trusts were originally looked upon as short-term bodies, early toll cottages were fairly primitive structures, and it was not until later in the 18th century that some trusts began to build sturdier toll houses, of which a few have survived along the Bath Road to this day. When the Chippenham Trust put up two new gates in 1744, two houses were rented for the keepers, who had only wooden shelters beside their gates.

Each trust usually erected two main gates placed at strategic positions across their piece or road, but not necessarily at either end. Their aims were to catch as many travellers as possible and to try to prevent them

The toll-house at Thatcham, built early in the 19th century and demolished in 1964

from taking alternative routes. Gates along the Bath Road were spaced out with several miles in between them, the distances being longer in country areas than around towns. Turnpike acts did not always lay down the position of gates, because the best position was sometimes only decided by trial and error, and sometimes other local considerations might make it necessary to change a gate's position. A good deal of gate moving took place, together with the erection of extra gates across side roads to discourage toll evasion. Few gates at the end of the turnpike era, in the 19th century, were in the same position as they had been when the trusts were first set up.

The Colnbrook trustees decided at their first meeting, on 1 June 1727, that a gate should be immediately erected across the road at the west end of Colnbrook near the road to Poyle, 'from or near the Bird in Hand to or near the smith's shop opposite'. Their second gate was west of Slough, near the Castle Inn at Salt Hill. The Maidenhead Trust had a gate at the western end of Maidenhead Bridge and one about a mile west of Twyford. The Reading to

Speenhamland Trust, in 1727, had one gate at the top of Castle Street on the western side of Reading, and one in Speen 'between the houses in the possessions of Jonathan Hicks and John White'. Later a gate was erected in Thatcham. The act for the Speenhamland to Marlborough Trust specified a gate on the section of road passing through the north of Kintbury parish, between the smith's shop and the lane leading to Ramsbury (i.e. the old road through Radley Bottom and Leverton) but this gate was later moved a mile to the east into Welford parish near the Halfway House. This trust also had a gate about 1½ miles west of Froxfield, near Harrow Farm. Their act forbade the erection of any turnpike gates within two miles of the town of Marlborough.

Beyond Marlborough, the Beckhampton Trust's main gate was in Beckhampton just before the Calne and Devizes roads divided. The Calne Trust had a gate on either side of the town, at Quemerford on the east, and near the Bremhill turning on the west. The Chippenham Trust had a main gate in the town centre and several other gates or bars on the outskirts of the town. The Bricker's Barn Trust erected a toll house and gate at Box when they opened their new route into Bath. On the Kingsdown road there was a gate and tollhouse at Blue Vein, where the tollhouse may still be seen. In Bath the city trust had a gate at Walcot, about a mile from the city centre. Many of these gates were later moved, and in addition, various other gates and side gates existed at different times along the Bath Road.

Tolls payable at these gates varied a little from trust to trust. A coach drawn by four or more horses was charged sixpence by the Reading to Speenhamland Trust, ninepence by the Speenhamland to Marlborough Trust, and one shilling by the Calne Trust. A wagon paid between sixpence and a shilling, according to the number of draught animals. Drovers paid five pence a score for oxen or cattle, and three pence a score for calves, sheep and pigs to the Reading Trust, and ten pence and five pence respectively for these animals to the Wiltshire trusts. One penny was the toll charged for a single horse, ass or mule by all three trusts. Pedestrians never paid toll and most trusts granted free passage to certain other road users. These included the royal family, soldiers on the march, post horses carrying mail, church-goers on Sundays, funeral processions, carriages on election days, carts carrying road mending materials, agricultural implements or manure, and horses going to water. In addition, special exemptions and arrangements were sometimes made to suit local interests. The Reading to Puntfield road act of 1746 contained clauses exempting carts or horses carrying cloth, serge or other woollen manufacture. Also exempt were the owners, occupiers and servants of Coley House and Farm, an estate bordering the Bath Road to the west of Reading, the main entrance to which was beside the turnpike gate. These were examples of protecting local trade, and of allowing inhabitants living within one mile of a turnpike gate to compound for an annual sum in lieu of tolls.

It can be seen that the tolls were designed to extract the most money from just those classes of road users who had formerly caused the most trouble for the parish authorities, and inflicted the heaviest wear on the roads – the long-distance coach and carriage travellers, goods waggons and droves of sheep, cattle and other livestock. Toll evaders, of course, were legion, and trust officers were hard put to it to catch dodgers and tricksters. Fines were imposed on landowners who allowed travellers to pass over their land in order to avoid toll gates; upon coach or waggon drivers who took off horses to reduce the amount of toll due; and upon persons forging or transferring tickets.

Toll evaders included a number of people who might have been expected to set a better example. In 1729, when it had been operating for more than two years, the Colnbrook Trust was obliged to remind some of its members that Trustees were not exempt from tolls, and that those who had not been paying were expected to make up arrears. Another evader was Mr. John Elwes, M.P. for Berkshire and a notorious miser, who habitually turned his horse aside from the highway and rode across country in order to bypass toll gates. 'Never pay a turnpike if you can avoid it', was his advice to an acquaintance (a magistrate) who once accompanied him on a journey.

Scales of charges were complicated by a mass of legislation regarding the weight carried by wagons, and the shape, height and breadth of wheels; all the regulations being designed to protect the road from the traffic. Trusts were empowered to set up weighing engines to check the weight of loaded wagons. Maidenhead Trust was one of the first to have such an engine. Its renewal act of 1728 ruled that 40 hundredweight should be the maximum load carried, and that a fine of 20 shillings should be the penalty for vehicles found to be overweight. Weighing engines became more common after 1740, and there were others at Colnbrook, Reading and Calne. These engines were huge cranes, rising high above the road, which actually lifted the wagon and its contents from the ground. They were costly to erect, required extra men to operate them and were often out of order. Colnbrook Trust minutes record a payment of 4 pounds 16 shillings for the repair of their engine in 1765, and a few years later the supernumerary gatekeeper was ordered to attend at the Colnbrook gate on three days and two nights each week, in order to assist in weighing wagons. Soon afterwards, a 'cistern' was made and set up over the engine to protect it from the wet.

Narrow wheels cut up road surfaces, so that new laws were frequently introduced requiring broader and broader wheels, effectively converting every heavy vehicle into a roller to flatten and consolidate the surface rather than cut it up. The famous Broad Wheel Act of 1753 required wagons to have wheels not less than nine inches wide, and those with narrower wheels were prohibited on turnpike roads. There were heavy fines for wagoners whose vehicles did not comply.

The job of turnpike gatekeeper was far from easy. His employers might put up a notice board at his gate stating the various tolls payable, but it was left to him to interpret

The sleeping gatekeeper

and enforce the complex regulations. He had to weigh wagons, measure wheels, count horses and livestock, check the type of goods carried, decide who was eligible for exemption, and collect money, including fines, from artful and sometimes abusive travellers. He worked long hours by day and night, in all weathers, and all too often his gate was situated on the outskirts of a town or on a lonely stretch of road, where he was an obvious target for highwaymen and footpads. The accommodation provided for him, especially in the early years, was spartan, as can be guessed from the comforts supplied by the trustees. In December 1732, for instance, the Colnbrook Trustees ordered their Surveyor to purchase a coat for each of the gatekeepers, and in 1738 a bed, a bolster and a rug were provided for the keeper at the Colnbrook gate.

In 1740 the same trust dismissed two gatekeepers on the same day, one for negligence and the other because he was 'incapable of performing his office'. Perhaps some idea of the nature of their offences can be gathered from the notice which the Clerk was ordered, at the same meeting, to put up at each gate, forbidding gatekeepers to allow anyone to sit tippling or gaming in either of the toll houses. In 1768 Benjamin Harvey, while on duty at the Colnbrook gate, was robbed of a silver watch which had cost him £2. 12s 6d. and 6s. 9d. of his own money. The Trustees paid him the full £2. 18s. 3d. in compensation, but three years later Harvey was dismissed, charged with having left his gate open several nights, so that carriages passed through without paying toll.

Dishonest gatekeepers were all too common. The isolated position of the gates and the impossibility of maintaining a full-time check on the tolls which had, or ought to have been, collected, unfortunately encouraged fiddling and 'private arrangements' with travellers. To make matters worse, the nature of a gatekeeper's work was hardly likely to make him a popular character, and pike-keepers, as they came to be called, acquired a reputation for rudeness and ill-temper. A 19th century government report described them as 'the most uncivil class of His Majesty's subjects'; while satirical prints showed the pike-keeper shivering in his night cap and shirt as he opened the gate for the night mail to sweep through, or being roused from his bed by impatient travellers hammering on his door and shouting 'Gate!'

Charles Dickens, writing at the very end of the coaching era, when the railway age was about to begin and turnpikes had nothing before them but years of debt and decline, left this description of the turnpike keeper, in the words of Tony Weller, the old coachman:

'They're all on 'em men as has met with some disappointment in life ... Consequence of vich, they retires from the world, and shuts themselves up in pikes; partly vith the view of being solitary, and partly to rewenge themselves on mankind, by takin' tolls.'

'Dear me,' said Mr. Pickwick, 'I never knew that before.'

'Fact, sir,' said Mr. Weller; 'if they was gen'l'm'n you'd call 'em misanthropes, but as it is, they only takes to pike-keepin'.'

5

Road Improvements

It is the worst public road in Europe, considering what vast
sums have been collected from it.
Gentleman's Magazine, September 1754.

By the time the 18th century moved into its third quarter,
turnpike trusts had become accepted as a necessary evil,
but the toll-paying traveller rightly expected something
for his money, and was not easily satisfied. Unfortunately
the science of road-making had advanced very little. The
vision, which perhaps some had shared with Defoe, of
roads comparable with those of the Romans, had faded.
The improved techniques which were to be developed by
Telford and McAdam were, as yet, undreamed of.

The critic writing in the *Gentleman's Magazine* in 1754
complained that road-makers 'who perhaps were
yeoman-like farmers and gentleman's bailiffs, made a
very poor figure in their undertaking; witness, amongst
others, that great road from London to Bath; it errs and
blunders in all the forms; its strata of materials were never
worth a straw; its surface was never made cycloidal; it
hath neither good side ditches, nor footpaths for walkers;
no outlets were made for water that stagnates in the body
of the road; it was never sufficiently widened, nor were
the hedges ever cleared – of course it is the worst public
road in Europe, considering what vast sums have been
collected from it.'

He was writing when the turnpiking of the Bath Road
had only recently been completed throughout its length,
and the various trusts and their surveyors still had much
to learn. About this time they were learning by trial and
error, for experiments were being carried out with a

variety of shapes and surfaces, aimed at solving the problem of draining water out of the road. The road laid wavy, with a continuous series of little hills and valleys; the angular road sloping like a pantile roof from one side to the other; the concave road, or hollow way, into which a stream was periodically turned to clean its surface; the built-up horizontal road, flanked by deep ditches, (sometimes a causeway from 20 to 30 feet wide, nearly horizontal on the top, with precipices on each side of four or five feet perpendicular depth) could all be seen, and experienced, on roads around London. Observation and comparison eventually led most trusts to decide that the best-shaped road was moderately convex, and artificially built up with small pebbles and gravel.

Trustees were also undertaking more widening and straightening of narrow and crooked sections of their road, improvements which involved cutting down trees and, here and there, the removal of a few humble cottages. Progress was being made.

In 1767 an observant and intelligent traveller along the Bath Road took the trouble to make copious notes and sent the following letter to the *Reading Mercury*. It was printed in the issue for 18 May.

Sir,   London, May 5, 1767.
    In a little excursion I made about five weeks ago from London to Marlborough, and back again in Post-Chaises, I took particular notice of the Turnpike road all the way; and as I have but little acquaintance with the Commissioners, I beg leave to convey a few observations to them by means of your paper.

The road from London to Reading is very good, and the Commissioners cannot be sufficiently praised, as they have widened it very judiciously in many places. I could only wish that they would consider the water just beyond Twyford; and if their tolls would allow it, would lay a sufficient quantity of gravel there, to raise the road above the floods, which so frequently overflow it, and make it broad enough for three carriages to pass by one another with ease. The water also at Cranford-bridge was so high at that time, that I was fearful it would have come into the chaise, in only getting to the little bridge, as the bar was down; but I was told that this is very uncommon. In some parts I observed that the gravel was loose and sandy, and wanted chalk, or some other cement to bind it.

From Reading to Newbury, the road is also in general very good; and I was assured that the Commissioners have lately widened it in many places, and at considerable expense. But I should think that the two little cottages at the further end of Theal, on the North-side of the road, should be pull'd down, and the ground they stand on be laid into the road to widen it; nor could the expense of purchasing them be a great deal. There is also another very narrow place just on the East-side of a stone barn a little on this side of Woolhampton, where a trifling sum would pay for cutting down a few trees, and laying a little of the field on the North-side into the road. But the principal place I would beg leave to mention, is a little beyond Ham-Mills, within a mile of Newbury, where the narrowness of the road between two ditches (one of which is very deep) makes it dangerous for two carriages to meet. How this may be amended in the best manner I can't say, but should think it best done, by filling up the deep ditch on the North-side, and adding 12 or 13 feet in breadth to the road, the whole length of that ditch. However, it is at present so very unsafe, that I hope something will soon be done to rectify it.

From Newbury to Marlborough, the road is very narrow in a great many places, but I doubt not but the laudable example which the Commissioners of the other turnpikes on the London road have set them, will also induce the gentlemen to widen these parts, as it is dangerous in many places to meet another carriage, but especially a broad-wheel'd waggon, many of which are continually travelling this road. The road also going down from the forest to Marlborough, I think still requires to be made broader; and if the hill could be rendered less steep, and consequently more safe, at a moderate expense, by removing some of the ground at the top of the hill, and laying it at the bottom, as has lately been done at Henley-on-Thames, it would be very desirable.

I observed, that in order to make the rain run off the quicker, they had in some places made the road rather too much upon the round to be quite safe. I write this the more feelingly, as I was very near being overturned in the post-chaise, by being obliged to turn out in one of those places for a broad-wheel'd waggon. This rounding should be done with prudence and moderation: but if the road was only to be widened, there would be no occasion to practise so disagreeable and dangerous a method.

I further took notice, that those mile-stones which were placed on the North-side of the road, and were thereby exposed to the heat of the sun all day, were generally more free from moss, and more plain and legible than those which stood on the South-side. And I should think, that if the numbers on them were to be in Arabic figures, instead of the Roman letters, they would be more easily read by the passengers, as the post-chaises pass by them very fast: thus for instance, 49 is more easily read than XLVIIII.

As it happened to be a rainy day when I returned home, I could not but pity the foot passengers I saw, who in many places were over their shoes in the dirt. Permit me, therefore, to recommend it to the consideration of the Commissioners of all the Turnpikes on the Bristol road, whether it would not be kind and humane, and of great advantage to all such honest sailors and other passengers as are obliged to travel this road on foot, to have the loose gravel laid up in a causeway under the hedge on the North side of the road, (as it would be sooner dry there after rain than on the South side) wherever there is no footway along the fields. And if this causeway was to be raised but three or four inches high in the narrow parts of the road, it would then be no obstruction to any carriage, if it should sometimes be obliged to run the wheels on one side upon it, when it meets with another carriage. This causeway must also have many little cuts made through it, to let the water run off from the road into the ditch, which cuts may be covered over with a flat stone.

I would also recommend it to the consideration of the drivers of every coach and carriage, whether when carriages of the same kind meet, it would not be advisable for each of them to take the right hand of the road, as it would prevent any disputes who should give way to the other.

I hope you will be so good as to print this in your next paper,

I am, Sir, Yours, etc.
J. Smith.

It is much to be regretted that J. Smith did not continue his journey all the way to Bath, so that we might have enjoyed his first-hand account of the state of the rest of the Bath Road. However, his letter is full of interest, not least in its assumption that the safety and speed of traffic should take priority over the environment. His recommendation that drivers should take the right side of the road when meeting other vehicles was not adopted; driving on the left became the recognised custom in this country, and was confirmed by the Highways Act of 1835. Inscriptions on milestones, it seems, were intended exclusively for gentlemen with a classical education. One wonders how many of the poorer travellers could read the place names, let alone the distances.

Apart from the road itself, so much of which survives today, milestones are the most potent reminders of the work of the turnpike trusts. Outside London they can still be seen nearly all the way along the Bath Road, and Mr Smith would doubtless be pleased to learn that the majority are on the north side. Some are barely legible, some are broken and half buried by road works, some have been moved from their original position or have vanished completely; others have been beautifully restored. They help to establish the route of the Bath Road in the 18th century, particularly where the modern A4 bypasses it. The inscriptions on them usually give the mileage to London, and to and from the nearest market towns. Some stones, between Maidenhead and Twyford, for example, state the distances from Hyde Park Corner

Milestones erected by four different trusts. a) Maidenhead Trust MS at
Knowl Hill, showing Roman numerals on the back b) Marlborough
Trust MS in Savernake Forest c) Beckhampton Trust MS on the east
side of Cherhill Hill d) Calne Trust MS, west side of Cherhill Hill

and Bath, thus confirming the importance of Bath as the western destination. The name of Bristol does not appear on the stones. At least one of the stones between Maidenhead and Twyford preserves, on its back, some Roman numerals, thus indicating that the stones were re-used when the present lettering and numerals were cut.

Of equal interest to the inscriptions are the different shapes and styles of the stones themselves. Each trust chose a distinctive shape, based on a combination of rounded, triangular and rectangular sections, designed to present to the eyes of the traveller two or three facets giving separately the distance to London, the distance from the last town passed through, and the distance to the next. By studying the shapes of the milestones it is possible to distinguish the lengths of road maintained by each trust. There is, for instance, a dramatic difference in shape between the milestones put up by the Speenhamland to Marlborough Trust and those put up west of Marlborough by the Beckhampton Trust. A different style again may be seen around Bath, where the Bath to Kingsdown Trust, among others in that area, had cast iron plates bearing the lettering fixed to the front of the stones.

Milestones began to be put up in the 1740s, when most turnpike acts included a clause requiring trusts to measure their roads and to set up stones stating the distances. Stones were certainly in position from Hyde Park Corner to Cranford Bridge early in 1740, for in the autumn of that year the Colnbrook Trust noted this fact and decided to follow suit. Their Surveyor was ordered to enquire of Mr Woodruff, stone mason of Windsor, or any other stone mason, what would be the cost of erecting stones of the same size along their own stretch of road from Cranford Bridge to Maidenhead. The first seven stones required were cut and erected in 1741, Roman numerals being used. The stone mason's bill came to £16. 16s. 0d, each stone costing £2. 8s. 0d. Labour and materials were cheaper in other parts of the country. When the Speenhamland to Marlborough Trust put up milestones in 1746, they paid only £1 each for them.

Milestones, like gates and other trust property, suffered from vandalism, so that it was necessary for turnpike acts to contain clauses making it an offence to pull up, break down or deface them. Time and the elements inflicted their own insidious damage, so that stones had to be replaced or recut every 30 years or so. Colnbrook's stones were all new faced and the letters recut and painted black in 1768. At the same time their Surveyor was ordered to put up milestones along the road which the trust had recently taken over from near the 18th milestone to Datchet Bridge (on the way to Windsor); and accordingly two new stones, numbered 19 and 20, were erected on the Datchet road. The Calne Trust, which erected milestones soon after 1744, had them all repaired in 1785. In the late 18th or early 19th century the Reading to Speenhamland Trust replaced some of its milestones with cast iron mileposts, and a few of these survive today.

Other road furniture for which trusts were responsible included direction posts at crossways, graduated posts where the road was subject to floods, lamps both at turnpike gates and in some towns (notably Colnbrook), and pumps for road watering. Some of the cast iron pumps remain.

The tradition that these pumps were put up by order of Beau Nash for the purpose of laying the dust for the benefit of travellers on their way to Bath, appears to have no foundation. There is no evidence to support it in any 18th century records concerning Nash or the Bath Road. Beau Nash died in 1761, and, for some years before his death, laws controlling gambling had reduced him to a state of near poverty. In the 1760s such road watering as was carried out was for the benefit of local residents rather than of passing travellers and was done by taking water from existing wells and streams. In May 1763 a complaint was lodged with the Colnbrook Trustees that the dust was 'very troublesome to the inhabitants', and the Surveyor was ordered to get a water cart made in order to water the town of Colnbrook. There are no

a   b

Bath Road pumps, a) in Longford b) in Twyford

references to pumps at that period. Four years later, the
following news item in the *Reading Mercury* of 25 May 1767
suggests that, even around London, the authorities were
only just beginning to organise an efficient system of road
watering.

> 'We hear that the first four miles of every road round
> town are to be lighted, watched, railed and watered;
> the expense of which is to be defrayed by the increase
> of toll that will arise in consequence of the
> improvement. The new method of watering the road,
> it is said, can be carried into execution at a fourth of the
> present expense, by pursuing the following regulation.
> At the end of every mile is to be a reservoir of water to
> fill the cart immediately, that the delay now in practice
> may be obviated. – The carts to contain four tons of
> water, to have double shafts and nine-inch wheels.'

The Brentford Trust, which maintained the road from Counter's Bridge (Hammersmith) to Cranford Bridge, commenced watering at this time, but it is difficult to establish when other trusts followed suit. Pumps were certainly in existence on the road near London by 1798, for in that year John Middleton, a Middlesex surveyor, reporting on the roads of that county, wrote that 'The turnpike roads ... are generally very bad; although at the toll-gates of this county there is collected a very large sum of money, probably not less than £30,000 a year, which is uselessly expended in sinking wells, erecting pumps, building carts, and hiring horses and men to keep the dust down by watering, instead of more wisely scraping if off. By the folly of this practice, the roads are kept many inches deep in mud; whereas if they were raked and swept clean winter and summer, there would neither be dust in such quantity as to offend nor any of the present obstructions. There is now double the draught necessary for conveying every carriage on the roads, along which there is no riding even in boots and horseman's coat during half the year. The mud indeed is so very deep all the winter and so fluid after rain as to render it unsafe to meet horses, owing to their feet throwing the mud not only over a horseman's clothes, but also into his eyes.'

The Colnbrook Trust, usually one of the more progressive of these bodies, apparently did not erect pumps until 1827, in which year their records refer to well-digging, purchases of bricks for lining wells, water carts, and to the expenditure of £759 for pumps made by Messrs Fowler & Co. The quality of these pumps has been proved by the fact that some fine examples still exist along the roads through Longford, Colnbrook and Datchet, maintained by this trust.

A few other pumps, in various stages of decay or preservation, survive along the Bath Road between Twyford and Thatcham, and many more existed into the early decades of the 20th century, but have disappeared as road widenings and alterations have taken place. Further west, pumps seem to have been less frequent, and none now survive on the road through Wiltshire or near Bath.

The records of the Calne Trust record only one pump, near the bridge at Quemerford, which was replaced by a new one in 1839, but this, too, has gone. Within living memory many old people could recall the pumps and water carts still in use until late in the 19th century. The cart had to be drawn from pump to pump at a speed nicely calculated to sprinkle the road sufficiently to lay the dust, but not so heavily that the cart was empty before the next pump was reached. Many old people could remember the delights of walking barefoot behind the cart on a hot summer's day.

By the end of the 18th century, long years of continuous maintenance and the useful experience gained by surveyors had resulted in much improved roads, allowing traffic to move more easily. But surveyors were still using large and small stones mixed indiscriminately for surfacing, and sometimes clay or chalk as well, with disastrous results. It was not until the second decade of the 19th century that the new techniques of Telford and McAdam began to be adopted; those of McAdam being widely used in the south and west of England. McAdam, who became Surveyor to the Bristol Trust, condemned all the old ways of road-making and argued that, instead of trying to make the traffic suitable for the road by innumerable regulations concerning widths of wheels and weights of loads, the road should be made strong enough to bear the traffic. He deplored the use of large stones in laying foundations, and insisted that, if the natural ground were made as dry as possible by efficient drainage, a firm, smooth road could be laid over it, using small, carefully graded stones. The top layer, composed of the smallest stones, would be ground down by the weight of iron-shod hoofs and wheels into a surface strong enough to bear the traffic and hard enough, with proper cambering, to drain off surface water. Once his methods had proved successful, and not too expensive, McAdam and his two sons were greatly in demand. By 1837 no fewer than 58 trusts were employing a member of his family.

Important and enduring works carried out by the trusts

were the many alterations to the line of the Bath Road, particularly those undertaken by the western trusts. In 1743 the Chippenham Trust began to consider improving the coach route to Bath via Chippenham. It was already maintaining the road from Studley Bridge into Chippenham but from there to Pickwick, where the coaches took the Lacock Trust's road from Sandy Lane to Kingsdown, was a stretch of unturnpiked road. In February 1743 they caused the Old Bath Road from Beckhampton to Pickwick, and their proposed new Bath road from the same two places running via Calne and Chippenham, to be measured. The old route was 16 miles 2 furlongs and 20 poles; the new route was shorter by 1 furlong and 16 poles. A year later they obtained an act enabling them to take over the road from Chippenham to Pickwick, and quarrying for stone to repair it began immediately at Derry Hill and Pickwick. What the Trust described as the New Bath Road was completed in 1745, and advertised as the best and shortest route for coaches. Undoubtedly it hastened the demise of the Old Bath Road as a coaching route.

But, still, travellers had to go via Chapel Plaister and Kingsdown for the last part of their journey to Bath, and it was not until after 1756 that another route was opened. In that year an act was passed, after lengthy opposition from landowners and existing trusts, allowing a more direct road to be built from the Cross Keys in Corsham through Hartham Park and Box to Batheaston Bridge. The act was obtained by a new trust named after Bricker's Barn, near the commencement of the new road. Slightly altered in 1828 to avoid Ashley Hill, the road now forms part of the A4.

In the last decade of the 18th century a new length of road was built at Cherhill Hill, hitherto one of the bleakest stretches of the Bath Road, as it then ran along the top of the hill instead of round the lower slopes, as it does today. Travellers, including those going by coach, had to toil up the steep ascent overlooking Cherhill village and along a mile or more of exposed hilltop before descending towards Beckhampton. In wet and windy

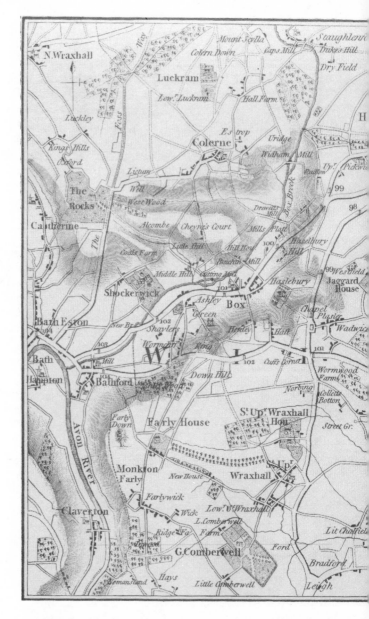

The Bath Roads from Chippenham to Bath, showing the Kingsdown and Box routes, about 1790

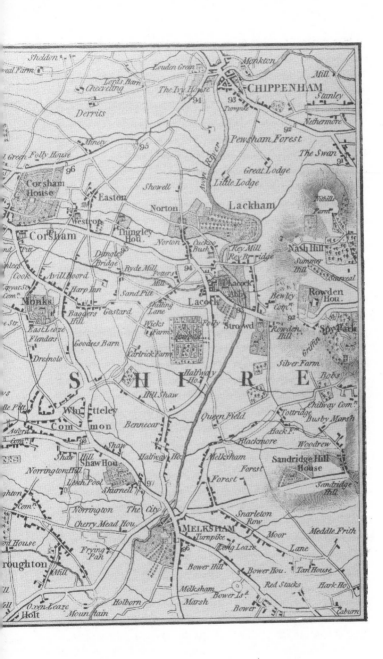

weather it could be a dangerous place; and in winter, snow could make the road impassable. Earth banks were thrown up by the turnpike trust to a height of about ten feet to provide protection from the weather and the worst buffeting of the winds, which were sometimes so strong that coaches were toppled over. One such incident was recorded in the *Bath Journal* of 12 February, 1770, in a letter from a gentleman living at Chippenham.

'Wednesday last between 1 and 2 o'clock as I was travelling on horseback near Beckington in Wiltshire, a storm of Wind and Snow blowing so violently I found it impracticable to proceed over the Down, therefore made the best of my way to Beckington house (Beckhampton Inn) where I was soon informed by some Gentlemen and 2 ladies, passengers belonging to two of the Bath Machines on their way to London, that they had undergone great distress in going over Cherhill Down; the storm overpowered the horses to such a degree, they would not go on; and in the Hurricane one of the Coachmen was blown off from his Box; this increased the fears of the Ladies and Gentlemen not a little; however they let down the windows of the Machines, to make way for the wind as it came sideways, to have a free passage through; and in this situation they sat near an hour, till they were almost perished with the cold; at length they determined to get out, to try to walk to Beckington house (the distance not being above a mile) but in consequence of this both Machines immediately overset, and the passengers were then in greater difficulties, being quite exposed to the inclemency of the wind and snow. One of the Gentlemen, in endeavouring to prevent the ladies from being quite blown away, lost his hold and was blown from his companions upwards of 150 yards, where he lay till assistance came to him, incapable of either seeing or hearing, and (according to the Gentleman's account of himself on his recovery from the fright) breathless. I stayed with these travellers above an hour and a half, and left the whole party recovered; and the storm being much abated, the people of the village and the coachmen were about getting their carriages off the Down, which they found impossible to attempt before.'

In 1787 the Beckhampton Trust, which maintained the road as far as the top of the hill, approached the Calne Trust with a proposal to build a new road, about two miles long, around the lower slopes of the hill on its northern side. This plan was eventually carried out, and the new road was opened in May 1792. The line of the old road can still be traced, by those who care to follow it, from the layby opposite the 82nd milestone from London, through a small copse and uphill to where the earth banks, overgrown with stunted bushes, can still be seen. The track is very rough, for in 1794 the Calne Trust removed the stones and other surface materials to use for repairing their roads elsewhere. Part of the western end of the old road has been ploughed up, but it rejoined the new road near the Bell Inn, now Bell Farm. Motorists today swoop up and down the gentle gradients of the road built in the 1790s.

About the same time the road to Bath via Devizes, which had become almost as popular a route for coaches as the Chippenham route, was lowered and straightened by the Devizes Trust. A new piece of road bypassed the old road running up to Shepherd's Shore, and led to the development of a new hamlet of that name on the low-level road. Between Calne and Chippenham the road was straightened, bypassing Derry Hill. These improvements were greatly appreciated a few years later during the severe weather of February 1799, when mail coaches on many routes were snowbound. The *Reading Mercury* reported that, notwithstanding the snow, the Exeter and Bath mails to London had been able to get through along the Bath Road, with the aid of six horses, and were arriving only three hours later than usual. 'So admirably is the business of travelling conducted on this road. The fall of snow has been much greater than any since the year 1776, when the communication was actually interrupted for several days; but the roads from Devizes, and from Calne to Beckhampton, have since been diverted from the hills into the level.'

6

Coaching on the Bath Road

From Hungerford we swift went o'er the Plain,
Too soon we came to the destructive Lane,
O fatal way! Here Rocks and craggy Stones
Our Limbs distorted, and unlock't our Bones,
The long worn Axle to the Coach, alack!
Gave here a dismal, unexpected crack.

From *A Journey to Bath and Bristol*. Anon. 1717.

By the time this comic-heroic poem was written, stage coaches were an accepted part of everyday life, and the middle-class travellers who used them took for granted the planned stages of the journeys, the availability of coachmen and horses, and the prearranged times of departure and arrival at inns. Less than a century before, such an organisation for public transport was unknown. The only conveyance then available for fare-paying passengers was the long, or stage wagon, a cumbersome vehicle drawn by eight horses, and covered with a hood, beneath which people and goods travelled together higgledy-piggledy at an average speed of two miles an hour. The first stage coaches appeared on the roads towards the middle of the 17th century, and were performing regular journeys, in the summer months at least, by the 1650s.

The earliest record of a stage coach service between London and Bath dates from 1657, when a London weekly newspaper called the *Public Adviser* announced in its issue for 19-26 May:

'Stage Coaches, Bath and Bristol. If any be desirous to go to Bath or Bristol let them repair to the sign of the Coach and 4 Horses at the lower end of Queen St. and there they may be furnished every Monday and Thursday with a Coach and Horses by Roger Bulbank and Henry Folbeg.'

Two weeks later the same newspaper announced that another coach service was running along the road to Bath:

'If any be desirous to go from London to Redding, Nubery, Marlbrough, Bath or Bristol, they may please to take notice that at the Red Lyon in Fleet Street, upon any Thursday, they may be accommodated with a Coach and 4 Horses to carry them to or from any of the said places at Reasonable rates by Onesiphorus Tapp of Marlbrough.'

By 1667 several coach proprietors were in competition and efforts were being made to speed up the journey, to limit the weight of luggage carried by pas ngers, and to keep to a more precise timetable. The following announcement appeared in *Public Advertisements* (which succeeded the short-lived *Public Adviser*):

'Flying Machine. All those desirous to pass from London to Bath or any other Place on this Road, let them repair to the Bell Savage on Ludgate Hill in London and the White Lion at Bath, at both of which places they may be received in a Stage Coach every Monday, Wednesday, and Friday, which performs the Whole Journey in Three Days (if God permit) and sets forth at five o'clock in the Morning. Passengers to pay One Pound, five shillings each, who are allowed to carry fourteen pounds weight; for all above to pay three half-pence per pound.'

Stage coaching very quickly became popular, and soon there were sufficient numbers of these vehicles on the roads for reaction to set in among those who objected to changes in the old ways of life, and feared that, if the lazy habit of coach riding grew widespread, the art of horse riding would be forgotten. Coaching was seen as a threat to health, to public morals, and to the livelihood of tradesmen such as saddlers and shoemakers, by a certain John Cresset, who in 1672 published a pamphlet pleading for Parliamentary control over the numbers of stage coaches.

'What advantage is it to Men's health', he argued, 'to be called out of their Beds into these Coaches an hour before day in the morning, to be hurried into them from place to place, till one hour, two, or three within night; insomuch that, after sitting all day in the summer-time stifled with heat, and choaked with the dust; or the Wintertime, starving and freezing with cold, or choaked with filthy Fogs, they are often brought into their Inns by Torchlight, when it is too late to sit up to get a Supper; and next morning they are forced into the coach so early, that they can get no breakfast? What addition is this to men's Health or Business, to ride all day with strangers, oftentimes sick, ancient, diseased Persons, or young Children crying; ... Is it for a Man's Health to travel with tired Jades, to be laid fast in the foul Wayes, and forced to wade up to the knees in mire; afterwards sit in the cold, till Teams of Horses can be sent to pull the Coach out? Is it for their health to travel in rotten Coaches, and to have their Tackle, or Pearch, or Axletree broken, and then to wait three or four hours (sometimes half a day) to have them mended again, and then to travel all night to make good their Stage?'

Cresset's eloquence went unheeded. Travellers, then as now, were prepared to put up with all kinds of delays and discomforts in order to reach their destinations; and even Cresset admitted that coach journeys were easier and encouraged people to travel more.

'These stage coaches make gentlemen come to London on every small occasion, which otherwise they would not do but upon urgent necessity; nay, the convenience of the passage makes their wives often come up, who, rather than come such long journeys on horseback, would stay at home. Then when they come to town they must presently be in the mode, get fine clothes, go to plays and treats, and by these means, get

List of coaches displayed at the King's Arms at Calne

such a habit of idleness and love of pleasure as makes them uneasy ever after.'

Within a few years there were coaches running every day of the week on all major routes. De Laune's *Present State of London*, 1681, listed these on the London to Bath and Bristol route:

Mr Saunders and Drews coach comes to the Chequers

near Charing Cross on Mondays and goes out on Tuesdays.

Robt. Tobys coach comes to the Swan near Somerset House on Wednesday and Saturday and goes out on Monday and Thursday.

Thomas Balden, Robt. Toby and Mr Booth come to the Bell in the Strand in the Summer time on Tuesday, Thursday and Saturday and go out on Monday, Wednesday and Friday.

Thomas Balden, Robt. Toby and Mr Booth come to the Talbot in the Strand on Wednesday and Saturday and go out on Monday and Thursday.

William Drews coach comes to the Angel in the Backside of St Clement's on Wednesday and Saturday and goes out on Monday and Thursday.

Although some coach services were run by coach or harness makers, many others were run by carriers and innkeepers. For the carrier it was a natural extension of his business; for the innkeeper it was a means of bringing regular custom to his inn. As there were a great many more inns on a busy route such as the Bath Road than were needed for stage coach purposes, other innkeepers could either persuade the coach proprietors to patronise their inns by offering special terms for stabling and accommodation, or set up in competition as coach operators.

One of the most successful coach proprietors on the Bath Road in the early 18th century was Thomas Baldwin, formerly a cooper in the City of London, and later landlord of the Crown Inn at Slough. The *Postman* for 10 May 1711 carried this announcement:

Bath and Bristol Flying Coach belonging to Thomas Baldwin at the Crown at Slough and to John Wilkenson of Bath, sets out from the Bell Inn in the Strand and the Saracen's Head in Friday Street and John Hunstores at the Chequers at Charing Cross on Mondays, Wednesdays and Fridays, London.

As the organisation of services improved, the time taken for the journey from London to Bath was reduced from three to two days, the two day coaches being called

Flyers. This speed had been achieved early in the 18th century and was largely due to the stationing of teams of fresh horses at suitably spaced inns along the road, instead of using, as the early coaches had done, the same tired horses for the whole journey, and making lengthy stops to rest and bait the animals.

Thomas Baldwin remained in business until 1726 and advertised in the London newspapers most years towards the end of April, when the 'Flying Season' started. His advertisements listed four or five picking-up places in London, and his coaches ran six days a week. In addition to the fast two day coaches, he ran a three day coach for people who preferred to travel in a more leisurely style. Two day coaches usually left at four o'clock in the morning, and three day coaches at six o'clock; passengers on the latter would also have been allowed longer stops at inns. Baldwin also made much of the fact that he employed the same coachman to drive a coach the whole distance from London to Bath and back again, and showed his flair for public relations by advertising his coachmen's names, 'John Baldwin, John Pinfolde, Anthony Somerhill and Henry Gardener.' Lesser coach services changed their drivers several times along the road, each driver naturally expecting a tip from the passengers. Baldwin's fares in 1725, the year in which he was able to start his summer services in the middle of March, were 22 shillings and 6 pence from London to Bath on a Flyer, and 20 shillings on the three day coach.

A stage coach usually held six, but occasionally eight, people. It was a heavy vehicle, built strongly to withstand the excessive jolting caused by the bad roads. The body, which was covered with stout leather nailed to the frame with broad-headed nails, was slung by massive leather braces from upright posts springing from the axletrees of the front and rear wheels. When the coach was in motion, the body swung from side to side, and lurched and shook as well when the coach wheels met a more than usually uneven patch of road. Only the hardiest travellers were not afflicted with nausea, and many were obliged to take to their beds for a day or two after a journey. Even so, the number of potential stage coach passengers was often greater than the number of available seats, and it was advisable to book in advance and to stay overnight at the inn, in order to board the coach in the morning.

A burlesque tale entitled *A Step to the Bath*, written by Ned Ward and published in 1700, gives some idea of how passengers stood up to the rigours of the journey. Ned and his companions, evidently hardened travellers, showed no interest in the passing scenery, but whiled away the long hours drinking and telling stories. His tale begins as the London season ends.

'The Town, and its Diversions, being grown as stale as a cast off Mistress ... and the Chiefest of its inhabitants withdrawn to their Rural Pleasures ... Necessity obliged me to make a country journey ... And the last summers expedition at Tunbridge-Wells not agreeing with my present Constitution and my inclination being bent after Novelties, I resolv'd to steer my course westward, to see what Pleasure those Pools of Iniquity called the Bath would afford me.'

Boarding a coach in an inn yard

Accordingly, he made his way to the Saracen's Head in Friday Street, and booked a place on Monday morning's coach. At dawn, he and his fellow passengers were summoned aboard their 'leathern conveniency' in which he complained, they were penned up like beasts in the Ark, and the journey began. 'Jehu tickled his cattle' and conveyed them in good time to Colnbrook, where they stopped at the George, 'an Inn famous for Extravagant Bills and Short Commons.' However, they had a good breakfast and re-entered their 'coop' for the drive to Reading, where they dined at the Mitre. After dinner the entertainment warmed up as they passed round a bottle of brandy, sang a few songs and told a lot more improbable stories. A few miles down the road they stopped again in Theale, for a restorative snack of 'Bottle Ale and Plumb-Cakes' at the sign of the Bell; then jolted slowly on to Newbury, the end of the journey for the first day. They put up at the King's Arms, and after supper Ned went for a walk in the dark and improved his acquaintance with a rich and vulgar widow who was travelling on the coach.

On the second day of the journey, all went well until they came to the 'Rocky Descent into Marlborough', where the coach was so violently thrown about that the brandy bottle currently circulating was shattered into a thousand pieces. This mishap provoked a good many hearty curses on the state of the road. In Marlborough they breakfasted at the Crown, where it transpired that the landlord was Mayor of the town; so Ned took the opportunity to complain bitterly about the 'Cursed Hill', demanding satisfaction for the damage they had sustained in breaking their brandy bottle, and saying that he would indict the whole Corporation unless speedy action was taken to repair the road. 'That we cannot do, Sir', replied the landlord, 'for in doing so we should Ruin half the Town; for the Damage that Hill occasions brings a considerable Trade to our Wheelwrights, Farriers and Chyrurgions; and also creates no small business to those of my own function, and maintains three or four families to support the coaches and assist at other accidents. But, however, I'll present you with a fresh cargo.'

Mollified by the landlord's gift of another sustaining bottle, the travellers left Marlborough and drove on across the Downs, where the grey wethers gave them a lot more 'confounded jolts' and they were alarmed to receive information that 'a party of Light Horse lay hidden, perchance to ease us of our Rino'. This news caused the widow to hide her purse of guineas in her petticoats and a Bristol merchant to shuffle all his guineas into the lining of his coat. Ned, whose pockets contained little to interest a thief, merely trusted to Providence. Fortunately the alarm proved false; no highwaymen attacked them, and they were able to recover their senses with liberal doses of brandy. At last they descended into the road leading to Sandy Lane, where the going was so deep in mud that it took three hours to cover two miles. After dining at the Bear, they proceeded on their way, 'but with a great deal of difficulty, for the Road was so Rocky, Unlevel, and Narrow in some places, that Ned was sure the Alps could be passed with less danger. At last, when they had almost given up hope of a safe arrival, they reached Bath, where the coach stopped at the White Hart. Here the merchant took a fresh coach for Bristol, and the others had supper at the inn and went in search of lodgings.

Next morning, being new arrivals in Bath, they were serenaded by the town waits; but either the standard of music had deteriorated since Pepys' day, or Ned had no taste for it, for he complained that 'we were saluted by the whole Fraternity of Cat Gut-Scrapers, and could not get rid of them without the assistance of an Angel.' A few days later, Ned and the rich widow were married.

In the anonymous poem, a little of which is quoted at the beginning of this chapter, the author presented a rather more romantic picture of a journey by stage coach to Bath, and took a little more notice of the places through which they passed. Again, the coach departed from the Saracen's Head, and the travellers set out before the sun had cleared the early morning mist. They stopped first at Turnham Green for a breakfast of spicy cakes and clear amber ale; and about eight o'clock they passed through the notoriously muddy town of Brentford, 'A famous place for Dirt and Water known.' At Slough they dined and enjoyed fine views of Windsor Castle. Beyond Maidenhead,

'We now came to the famous Woods of old,
Where Trav'llers often lose their darling Gold,
Where cunning Thief with a tremendous Hand,
From thicket Rushes, bids the Coachman Stand.'

In spite of this dramatic build-up, they drove through the Thicket unmolested and arrived at Reading, where they had wine, brandy and a cold repast, which the coach's time schedule obliged them to consume hurriedly. Next, 'fair, spacious Newbury' was reached, and they enjoyed a delicious supper; for 'tender chickens and rarest fish, Trout and eel here in perfection are.' On the following day they passed through 'marshy Hungerford that's famed for Beer', and, not long afterwards, came to the deep, rough road leading into Marlborough which seems to have had as bad a reputation as any part of the Bath Road. It was then that disaster struck:

'The long worn Axle to the Coach, alack!
Gave here a dismal, unexpected crack.'

The passengers were flung all over the coach, but managed to clamber out and, having inspected the damage, made their own way on foot into Marlborough, where they waited at an inn until the coach had been repaired and caught up with them. After this delay, the coachman had to make up for lost time, so they travelled as fast as they could over the Downs to Beacon Hill, where they paused, perhaps to allow the horses to breathe, and the travellers admired the famous view of the vale and the historic town of Devizes. The remainder of the journey was uneventful, and they arrived safely in Bath for the night.

On both of these early 18th century journeys the coach went by way of Shepherd's Shore and Sandy Lane. This was the recognised coach route at that time and for some years to come. The Bear Inn, where Ned Ward and his companions dined, was a famous inn and the regular stopping place for stage and private coaches. A good dinner could be depended upon there, and it was widely known for a special kind of pudding, called Sandy Lane Pudding.

Sandy Lane, as one traveller recorded, was so named because it was a long lane of deep sand which could be very trying for travellers on dry windy days. It came between two long steep hills – Bowden and Beacon – which were notoriously dangerous, hard on horses and difficult to maintain. Beacon Hill was particularly bad, and extra horses often had to be hired to help drag coaches up to the top. Once this was reached, several miles of bleak downland lay ahead, where travellers were exposed to the worst of the weather, and the dangers of being overturned or robbed. Promoters of the alternative route through Chippenham, which was being developed by a rival trust, lost no opportunity of drawing attention to the perils of the Sandy Lane route, and in defence of the latter the following notice was published in the *London Evening Post* of 24 March 1737.

'They write from Kennet in Wilts that since last November upward of 200 coaches have gone the lower road leading from Sandy Lane through Beckhampton to and from Marlborough in the way to Bath and Bristol and that no coach hath been overturned, robbed or lost their way. They further add that Thirty Brakes are now made in it and that the whole Way except about half a mile is a double road, but the Coachmen and some Publicans whose interest is reverse to the Public good do falsely aver that this road is confined and impassable.'

The promoters of the Old Bath Road, however, were fighting a losing battle. The Chippenham Turnpike Trust, already benefiting from the volume of traffic passing through that town on the way to Bristol, was able to carry out improvements over rather less difficult terrain than that crossed by the Old Bath Road. After they had taken over an additional stretch of road between Chippenham and Pickwick, this notice appeared in the *Bath Journal* of 9 September 1745.

'This is to inform the Publick. That the new Road

leading from Beckhampton near Marlborough in Wiltshire (through Calne and Chippenham to Pickwick in the same County) is now completely finished: whereby persons travelling from London to Bath and Bristol may avoid Bowden and Bagdon (i.e. Beacon) Hills, too well known and dreaded by Travellers to need description. This is also the nearest and the Post Road: and during the Summer Season will be rendered more than ordinary pleasant by the use of Stanley and Studley Commons, by which the length of the way will be considerably shortened, and Coaches, etc., may keep the turf for four or five miles together. On this road also are most convenient Watering Places every Two or Three Miles throughout the whole, Advantages it is known the Sandy Lane has not.'

In spite of all the advantages of the new road, many private coach travellers, horsemen and others who enjoyed the fine, clear air and open views over the Downs, remained faithful to the old road, and to the Bear Inn at Sandy Lane, for some years longer. When the Princess Caroline visited Bath in the spring of 1746 she dined at Sandy Lane on her way back to London; and again, in April 1750, when she visited Bath, Beau Nash went as far as Sandy Lane to meet her. But the public coach services very soon transferred their custom to the Chippenham road. The proprietors of the London Stage Coach announced in the *Bath Journal* of 18 June 1750 that

'The London Stage Coach in Three Days (from Mr Pinfold's at the Bell Inn in Bath every Monday and Thursday) Now goes through Chippenham and Calne and not the Sandy Lane Road. The Passengers dine at the Angel Inn at Chippenham.'

The speedier two day coaches had probably changed routes long before this.

Toll receipts at gates on the Sandy Lane road fell disastrously. In 1735 they amounted to £204; in 1751 a mere £78. The trustees met in May 1755 to consider the situation and, finding it hopeless, decided to abandon the road. It was still usable, however, for many years, and Cary's *New Itinerary*, the standard travellers' guide to

81

roads, coaching routes and inns throughout the late 18th and early 19th centuries, continued to list the Sandy Lane road until 1817, but omitted it from later editions. After 1750 the turnpiking of the lower roads through Devizes and Melksham opened up an easier route which became a popular alternative to the Chippenham route in the busiest years of the coaching era.

As the turnpike system developed and more roads were improved for wheeled traffic, the number of stage coach services increased until an efficient network covered nearly the whole country. The clumsy black leather-covered coaches of the early period gave way to beautifully built and better sprung vehicles whose bodies and wheels were painted in the bright colours belonging to their owners, and bore on their side panels the device of the inn from which they operated and the names of the towns between which they ran. Although mud and dust often rendered them less gleaming than they appear in coaching prints, they must still have been a sight to make the countryman stand and stare as they passed along the roads.

At the height of the coaching era, in the 1820s and 30s, nearly 700 long-distance coaches set out every day from the city of London for all parts of Britain. Over 20 ran to Bath and Bristol, while several others ran as far as Maidenhead, Reading or Newbury. Many other coaches ran intermediate journeys.

At this time, most long-distance coaches were owned by big London-based firms operating from coaching inns in the City. The most successful coach proprietor, William Chaplin, owned and ran his coaches from the Swan with Two Necks in Lad Lane, Cheapside. As his business grew, he acquired also the White Horse in Fetter Lane, and the Spread Eagle and Cross Keys, both in Gracechurch Street. At the Swan with Two Necks, an ancient inn with a galleried yard approached down a narrow lane, he increased his capacity by building underground stabling for 200 horses beneath the yard. At Hounslow, the first stop out of London for nearly all the westbound coaches, he owned stables for a further 100 horses. Chaplin's coaches were usually painted red and black – black upper quarters and fore and hind boots, and red wheels and underparts – and bore the device of the Swan with Two Necks, or that of his other inns. His business, which included his own horse buying and veterinary departments and ownership of several hotels, gave employment to 2,000 people. His fast named coaches, the Manchester Defiance, Birmingham Greyhound, Cambridge Telegraph, Liverpool Red Rover, Cheltenham Magnet and Bristol Emerald, became household names.

Other proprietors with coaches running along the Bath Road were Robert Gray, who operated from the Bolt-in-Tun, Fleet Street, and ran 25 coaches along the southern and western roads; Mrs Sarah Ann Mountain of the Saracen's Head, Snow Hill, who had her own coach factory behind the inn and, in addition to her own 30 coaches, hired out vehicles to other operators at the rate of 3½d per mile; and Benjamin Horne, whose base was the Golden Cross, Charing Cross, (on the site of Nelson's Column); he also owned the George and Blue Boar, Holborn, and the Cross Keys, Wood Street.

Most large inns ran post coaches, which were lighter and faster than the ordinary stage coaches. They carried four passengers and higher fares were charged for the speedier journey. Post and stage coaches are included in this list of daily departures from London to Bath in 1828.
A.M.
5.00 The Regulator, through Marlborough, Calne and Chippenham, from the Spread Eagle, Gracechurch Street, and 220 Piccadilly.

6.00 The Triumph, through Calne, from the Angel, St Clement's.

6.00 A coach from the White Bear, 221 Piccadilly. (Not Sundays).

6.15 The Company's Day Coach in 12½ hours, through Marlborough and Chippenham, from the White Bear, Basinghall Street.

6.15 York House Company coach, through Calne and Chippenham, from the Belle Sauvage, Ludgate Hill.

6.45 The Emerald, through Marlborough and Devizes, from the Spread Eagle, Gracechurch Street, and 220 Piccadilly.

7.00 The Company's Day Coach in 12½ hours, from the Old White Horse Cellar, Piccadilly.

8.00 Gray's coach, through Chippenham, from the Bolt-in-Tun, Fleet Street.

8.00 Horne's coach from the Golden Cross, Charing Cross.

P.M.

1.00 A coach from the Black Lion, Water Lane.

1.00 A Post Coach in 12 hours, through Calne and Chippenham, from the White Horse, Fetter Lane.

1.00 A Post Coach in 12 hours, from the Saracen's Head, Snow Hill.

1.00 The Blue, through Marlborough, Calne and Chippenham, from the George and Blue Boar, Holborn. (Not Sundays).

1.30 A coach from the White Bear, 221 Piccadilly. (Not Sundays).

3.00 A coach from the Black Lion, Water Lane.

4.00 A Post Coach in 12 hours, from the Swan with Two Necks, Lad Lane.

4.30 The Regulator, through Devizes, from the Cross Keys, Wood Street.

4.30 Gray's coach, through Chippenham, from the Bolt-in-Tun, Fleet Street.

4.30 The Company's Night Coach, through Devizes and Melksham, from the White Bear, Basinghall Street.

5.00 The Monarch, through Chippenham, from Gerard's Hall, Basing Lane, and the Belle Sauvage, Ludgate Hill.

5.00 Horne's coach, from the Golden Cross, Charing Cross.

5.00 The Shamrock, from the Spread Eagle, Gracechurch Street, and 220 Piccadilly.

7.30 Bath and Bristol Royal Mail, through Devizes, in 12¾ hours to Bath, and 14¼ hours to Bristol, from the Swan with Two Necks, Lad Lane. Leaves at 7.00 on Sundays.

The coaching business soon outgrew the accommodation at inns. Booking offices moved out into nearby premises, and stables were built on plots of land on the outskirts of towns. The largest stabling centre in the country was at Hounslow, where at the height of the coaching age over 2,000 horses were stabled. Hounslow was customarily the end of the first stage out of London and, on return journeys, the last place where the west country coaches changed horses before reaching their city termini. The supply and care of horses was big business, and a coach proprietor's heaviest expense. Work on the fast coaches was strenuous in the extreme, and horses had to be replaced after three years' service. In the earlier, less hectic period of coaching they had been expected to haul a coach for 10 or 11 miles in a day, and back again over the same road in the next. But as roads improved and coaches speeded up, the horses were made to run a six or seven mile stage out in the morning and back again later in the day. Many coachmen objected to this practice, but it was said to have the advantage that the horses were always cared for in their own stables. At the end of their three year stint the horses were sold off through dealers or newspaper advertisements, and the lucky ones lived out their lives more comfortably as farmers' or tradesmen's horses. The unlucky ones were those killed or maimed in the numerous coaching accidents, or which belonged to mean, brutal proprietors who worked them on the coaches until they literally died in harness.

One of the most tragic events of the coaching age was a fire which broke out one night in February 1835, when 35 horses used on the Bath and Bristol stage coaches were burned to death. It happened at a stabling establishment in the London Road at Reading (on the site of the Royal Berkshire Hospital). The fire started soon after the Age Bristol coach had left for London, and this being the last due that night, the two men in attendance locked the stables and went home, having, as they claimed, carefully extinguished the lantern. But a spark from the wick was generally believed to have set fire to the straw. The thatched roof was soon alight and collapsed into the stables. The alarm was raised by people living on the opposite side of the road, but nothing could be done to save the horses, all of whom died a horrible death. There was tremendous sympathy for what the newspapers called 'these useful and unoffending servants of man', and when it was afterwards suspected that the fire had been started as an act of revenge upon the owner, it was condemned as 'the atrocious and inhuman act of a monster.'

Public transport represented only a minor proportion of the numerous vehicles seen on the roads in the late 18th and early 19th centuries. Many people travelled privately in their own or hired vehicles. Travel was essential to the new, urbanised way of life then developing, and fewer people continued to live their lives entirely in the country.

Business and industry, art, education and amusement were concentrated in the towns and cities, and thither everyone, for one reason or another, had to travel. In response to demand, various new types of vehicle were introduced to suit the requirements of those who could, and those who could not, afford their own facilities. The rich kept their own coaches, and as coach-building improved, comfortable light travelling carriages took the place of the clumsy vehicles which had formerly lumbered along the roads. Vehicles were invented which, by making certain adjustments, could be converted from town coaches into travelling carriages. The coachman's seat and footman's perch, used on short town journeys, could be replaced by a coachman's box containing luggage space, and a rear boot on top of which the footman rode in a rumble or dickey seat. The owner then travelled with his own servants, and hired at posting inns fresh teams of horses at every stage of the journey. The hired horses would be accompanied by a postilion, riding the near-side lead horse, and he would be responsible for returning them to the inn which employed him. Other town coaches could be converted for use without a coachman, replacing his box with a large luggage boot.

Post-chaise travellers in difficulties

The traveller was then entirely dependent upon a postilion to drive him over each stage. In both cases the rich could make long journeys in the comfort of their own carriages, and without having to use their own horses.

People who did not have their own coaches, but could afford to pay for more comfort and privacy than were offered by the stage-coaches, travelled in hired post-chaises (small closed carriages for two passengers and a limited amount of luggage) which could be had at posting inns along with a postilion and horses. This class of traveller included large numbers of lesser gentry and well-to-do business and professional men. The posting service was well organised and could take a traveller from one end of the country to the other. Post chaises, often painted yellow and known as 'yellow bounders' were among the commonest vehicles on the roads, far outnumbering stage-coaches. Postilions often wore bright yellow jackets, to match the chaises, with breeches, short top boots and beaver hats. Each postilion had four horses in his charge, and used his first and second pair in turn. At every efficient posting inn at least one postilion would be ready with a pair of horses, so that there would be the minimum delay when the next customer arrived.

The system, known as 'travelling post', had developed out of the connection between inns and the Post Office, when certain innkeepers, as part of their remuneration for acting as postmasters, were licensed to hire out horses to travellers. By the middle of the 18th century the hire of post-horses and chaises made up a very substantial part of the innkeeper's livelihood, and in towns where there was more than one posting inn, keen competition usually existed between them. Sometimes innkeepers in neighbouring towns got together to advertise chaise hire at the various stages along a main road, as can be seen in this advertisement published by innkeepers along the Bath Road in 1755.

POST-CHAISES

Mary Dalrymple at the Angel Inn at Marlborough, William Mackelary at the King's Arms Inn at Speenhamland, and James Askue at the King's Arms Inn at Reading, beg leave to inform the Nobility, Gentry, and others, that may have occasion to travel the Bath Road, that they furnish good Four and Two-Wheel Post-Chaises, and able Horses, at the following prices, viz:

	Two-Wheel	Four-Wheel
From Reading to Salt Hill	10s. 0d.	14s. 0d.
From Reading to Maidenhead	7s. 0d.	10s. 0d.
From Speenhamland to Reading	9s. 0d.	13s. 0d.
From Speenhamland to Marlborough	10s. 0d.	15s. 0d.
From Marlborough to Chippenham	10s. 0d.	15s. 0d.

In the same newspaper four rival innkeepers – Richard Fisher at the Crown in Reading, John Carey at the Pelican, Speenhamland, George Smith at the Castle, Marlborough, and John March at the Orkney Arms,

Maidenhead Bridge – announced that they too ran post-chaises along the same stages at the same charges, with Mr March charging 12s. 0d. or 8s. 0d. for the distance from Maidenhead to Hounslow.

In the Regency period, skill in driving a coach and handling a team was something to which every gentleman aspired, from the undergraduates who bribed stage-coachmen to let them drive the coaches (causing many accidents) to the more mature gentlemen whose enthusiasm led to the formation of the Bensington Driving Club, in 1807, and the Four Horse Club in the following year. Members of the exclusive B.D.C. drove twice every year to Bensington (or Benson) in Oxfordshire, where they dined at the White Hart and drove home by lamplight, or in the early hours of the next morning. The regular run of the Four Horse Club was along the Bath Road as far as Salt Hill.

The Four Horse Club held its first meeting in April 1808, and met thereafter on the first and third Thursdays in May and June at the house of its president in Cavendish Square. From there members drove their smart light coaches, drawn by teams of glossy, high-bred horses, through Kensington to Turnham Green where a stop was made at the Packhorse Inn. A luncheon for 30 was always laid out ready for them, and traditionally they drank cider cup made with hock and borage. The drive continued to Hounslow Heath, where similar refreshments awaited them at the Magpies. At Salt Hill they dined alternately at the Windmill or the Castle Inn, and each inn stabled the horses which the other could not accommodate. No strangers were admitted during these dinners, and the proceedings usually grew fairly riotous. The horses had a rather less enjoyable excursion than their drivers, for they ran the whole distance of 24 miles to Salt Hill, and back the next day, without being taken out of their harness. The Four Horse Club ceased to exist about 1826. The B.D.C. survived until 1854.

7

Royal Mail

The London Mail did not arrive here till near five Hours after the usual Time last Monday morning, owing to the Postman's getting a little intoxicated in his Way between Newbury and Marlborough, and falling from his Horse into a Hedge, where he was found asleep by Means of his Dog. *The Bath Journal*, 5 November 1770.

Bath in the 18th century was the home of two famous reformers of the postal system, Ralph Allen and John Palmer. When that century opened, letters were carried, neither expeditiously nor very safely, by postboys on horseback; when it closed, they were transported by a fast and efficient mail coach service.

The postal system dated back to the reign of Charles I when, in order to raise revenue for the royal purse, the Crown postal service, which carried royal and official letters and documents, was thrown open to the general public on payment of postage based on a scale of fixed charges for distances. Previously, a few letters had been carried unofficially by the royal post but most letters had travelled by private messengers or on the packhorses and wagons of common goods carriers. In 1635 a Chief Postmaster was appointed, who immediately set about establishing a complete system of posts for public use on the six main post roads of the country, with branch posts to all important towns off the main routes. The main post roads radiated from London to Dover, Plymouth, Bristol, Holyhead for Ireland, Edinburgh and Yarmouth. Post roads were divided into stages of between 10 and 15 miles in length, and at the end of each stage a post house was set up, where horses were kept in readiness to carry the mail over the next stage. A post house was usually a town inn. The innkeeper received a small fee for his services as postmaster, together with the more remunerative right to hire out horses to travellers along the post road.

Postmaster–innkeepers were required to hang out the sign of a post horn, the instrument used by postboys carrying the mail to give warning of their approach. The sign also served as an indication to travellers of a post house. On the London to Bristol road there were post houses at Hounslow, Maidenhead, Reading, Newbury, Marlborough, Chippenham and Bath. Branch routes ran from Maidenhead to Oxford, Gloucester and South Wales; and from Marlborough to Devizes and other Wiltshire towns.

Postmasters were responsible for providing horses, checking and recording the packets of letters in the mail bag and forwarding them along the main or branch post roads, delivering or retaining for collection letters which arrived for their own post town areas, and collecting any postage which might be due. Postage was rarely paid in advance because it was felt that the Post Office would take more care of a letter if the postage had to be collected from the recipient. Letters to inferiors were usually prepaid.

Most long-distance letters had to travel up one main post road to London, where they were recorded at the General Post Office, and down another to their destinations, but in the 17th century cross-posts, providing more direct and cheaper routes began to develop. Two official ones linked Exeter with Chester and Bristol with Oxford, but there were many unofficial ones set up by country postmasters and operated largely to their own advantage. As the General Post Office had no effective means of checking the letters passing along these routes it was all too easy for country postmasters to make their own arrangements and to pocket a large part of the revenue. The same facility for fraud existed in the handling of bye-letters, the letters intended for local delivery or which needed to travel only part of the way along a post road. The result was that, as the volume of public correspondence increased, so did the income of country postmasters; but the General Post Office was deprived of a substantial part of its revenue.

These, and other malpractices, were the subject of a report in 1677 called A General Survey of the Post Office, which recommended that surveyors be appointed to ride along all the post roads, checking the work of postmasters and postboys, and keeping a watch on the numbers of bye-letters at each stage. No action resulted from this report, and it was not until 1715 that six surveyors, one for each main post road and its branches, were appointed to examine post office accounts and the management of the postal services. Their findings so impressed, or appalled, the Postmasters General that their Lordships were all the more willing to consider the proposal put before them by Ralph Allen, the young and ambitious Postmaster of Bath. Ralph Allen was the son of a Cornish innkeeper, and while a boy he had often stayed with his grandmother who kept the post office at St Columb, and assisted her with the accounts. By 1719 he was Postmaster of Bath, and although only 26 had several years of experience behind him and an extensive knowledge of the activities of dishonest postmasters who managed bye- and cross-posts. He offered to pay £6,000 a year for the contract for the bye- and cross-posts 'between Exeter and Chester, and all the towns between those places, and also the road between Bristol and Oxford, going by way of Bath, Wantage and Abingdon', he himself being entitled to all the revenue he might receive above that sum. £6,000 was half as much again as the estimated annual value of those posts, and the Postmasters General, who had never succeeded in making them pay, agreed to give him the contract for a period of seven years.

For the first few years Allen made a loss, but when he had the situation fully under control his success, and his own fortune, were assured. By exercising, through his own surveyors, strict supervision over all postmasters and postboys on his routes, and devising systems of checking on all letters sent and delivered, he made the posts not only more profitable but speedier and more reliable. In addition, he set up many new cross-post routes and increased the frequency of deliveries from every other day to daily. His contract with the Post Office was regularly renewed, and for increasingly large areas; while his annual payment to that department trebled to over £18,000.

Ralph Allen became a very wealthy man, a leading citizen and generous benefactor of Bath. He purchased land on Combe Down on which was a very profitable quarry supplying large quantities of the stone used in the rebuilding and expansion of Bath which was then taking place. Near his quarry, John Wood the elder built for him the splendid classical mansion of Prior Park, which served him as a country home and as the headquarters of his business concerns. Above the coach house were the offices from which his surveyors operated, keeping watch over the post routes under his control. At Prior Park he entertained his friends, among whom were some of the most distinguished writers, artists and actors of his time. Pope, Fielding, Richardson, Gainsborough, Hoare, Garrick and Quin were among his long-staying guests.

He died in 1764, leaving the postal services greatly improved in many ways but still dependent for transport on postboys mounted on indifferent horses or, on busy routes, driving mail carts. Postboys, who were sometimes boys and sometimes fully grown men, had always been a source of trouble. Despite the Post Office rule that the mails must be carried at a speed of not less than seven miles an hour in summer and five miles an hour in winter, 'as the ways afford and the weather fall out', such speed was rarely maintained. Complaints were made about postboys loitering on the roads, tippling at alehouses, pocketing money for carrying letters and performing errands which were no part of their duties, lending their horses, neglecting to blow their horns, pilfering from the mail bags, and even being in league with highwaymen and footpads. On their behalf it was acknowledged that they were badly paid and that their work was arduous, tedious and often dangerous. Postmasters, retaining the better horses in their stables for private hire, mounted the postboys on worn-out hacks; and yet they were expected to carry the mails at a steady speed in all kinds of weather, enduring biting frosts, drenching rains, dense fogs and blinding snow. Sometimes, on reaching the end of their stages, they were so numb with cold that they had to be lifted from their saddles; and there were instances of postboys being swept away in floods and frozen to death in snowdrifts. Perhaps worst of all, the letters they carried often contained bank notes for considerable sums, making them a favourite target for robbers. Attacks of this nature became so frequent that the Post Office advised people to cut bank notes into two and send the halves by different mails, waiting to hear of the receipt of the first half before despatching the second. The public, however, considered the mails so unsafe that they resorted to disguising their letters as parcels and sending them by stage coach. This was illegal as well as more expensive, but widely practised.

Nearly 20 years after the death of Ralph Allen another enterprising citizen of Bath put forward a plan for the speedier and more secure conveyance of the mails. John Palmer was the son of a wealthy Bath brewer with interests in the theatre. He was manager of the theatres in Bath and Bristol, obtaining for both the royal patent, and his work required frequent rapid journeys between those cities and London. He observed that, while the mail which left London on Monday night did not arrive at Bath until Wednesday afternoon, he himself accomplished the journey by fast stage coach in 17 hours. As a businessman, he fully understood the importance of speedy communications. He saw that, while the rest of the world was moving faster along better-made roads and by better organised coach and carrier services, the post, which should be the fastest conveyance, was as slow as ever.

The plan he put forward was that the mails should be carried by coach. Contracts could be placed with coach proprietors for their conveyance at the rate of threepence per mile, the same rate as the Post Office was then paying for a boy and horse. Each coach should be guarded and should carry no outside passengers. The guard, who must be skilled in the use of firearms, should sit on the top of the coach with the mail behind him, so that he could command the road and be always on the watch for suspicious persons. He was to be armed with two blunderbusses, and the coachman with two pistols. A speed of eight or nine miles an hour was to be maintained so that, stoppages included, the distance from London to Bath could be covered in 16 hours, an hour less than the fastest stage coach and very considerably less than the 38 hours usually taken by the postboys. In order to achieve this speed, the horses were to be changed more frequently, about every six miles, and the length of time of stoppages reduced. When the coach arrived at the end of each stage, the postmaster was to be waiting to receive the mailbag, remove the incoming letters and put in the outgoing ones. Fifteen minutes should be ample for this purpose and for changing the horses. The coaches must run to a strict timetable, and if one of them was late arriving a man on horseback should be sent to find out the cause of the delay.

It was fortunate for Palmer that, in 1782, he was able to secure an introduction to William Pitt, then Chancellor of the Exchequer, and win his support for this revolutionary plan. The Postmasters-General and all their District Surveyors were strongly opposed to it, and in the months that followed produced three volumes of objections, claiming that it was absolutely impracticable and prejudicial to revenue and commerce. Palmer, of course, was regarded as an ignorant outsider with no understanding of the working of the Post Office. Surveyors in all districts declared that the existing system was as perfect as it could be. They were amazed to learn that there was any desire for change, and could see no reason why the post should be the swiftest conveyance in England.

In 1783, while all these objections were being raised, Pitt was out of office, but Palmer was undeterred and devoted the time to perfecting his plan. Relinquishing his theatrical interests, he travelled the length and breadth of the kingdom by stage coaches, noting down journey times, fares, arrangements for changing horses, ways in which time was lost unnecessarily, and how the coaches could be better regulated for carrying the mails. At the same time he acquainted himself with all the postal routes, carefully observing their defects and causes of delay. Meanwhile, in Bath and Bristol, he employed people to watch the coaches as they set out for London and to count the number of parcels which appeared to contain letters. He was assured that the number amounted to several hundreds every week, all representing a loss of revenue to the Post Office.

In 1784 Pitt was back in office and still in favour of Palmer's plan. At a meeting held at the Treasury on 21 June, he over-ruled all Post Office objections and ordered a trial to take place. An experimental run was to be made, at Palmer's expense, along the London to Bath and Bristol road. This road was chosen not only because it was Palmer's home route but because it was in much better condition than any other main post road.

The trial was to last a week, commencing on Monday 2 August. Palmer, having so much information at his fingertips, was able to complete all the arrangements by the end of July, and on the 31st of that month five innkeepers signed an agreement to provide horses for the coach at short stages along the road in consideration of a payment of threepence per mile. Of the five innkeepers, one was in London, one in Thatcham, one in Marlborough, and two in Bath. Wilson, the then proprietor of the Swan with Two Necks in Lad Lane, horsed the coach for 11 miles from London to Brentford. From there, it was horsed for the next 46 miles by Fromont of the King's Head at Thatcham; and from Thatcham to Calne, a distance of 34½ miles, by the Marlborough innkeeper (whose name seems to be unknown). From Calne, the Bath innkeepers took over for the Bath and Bristol stages. One of these was probably Williams of the Three Tuns, who was co-proprietor with Wilson in London of the coach used on the trial journey.

This vehicle was no smart new turn-out but an ordinary diligence, a light coach normally drawn by two horses, and used on short-distance runs.

On 29 July 1784 the proprietors inserted this announcement in the *Bath Chronicle*.

'Mail Diligence, to commence Monday, August 2nd. – The Proprietors of the above carriage having agreed to convey the Mail to and from London and Bristol in sixteen hours with a Guard for its protection, respectfully inform the Public that it is constructed so as to accommodate four Inside passengers in the most convenient manner, that it will set out every night at eight o'clock from the Swan with Two Necks, Lad Lane, London, and arrive at the Three Tunns, Bath, before ten the next morning and at the Rummer Tavern near the Exchange, Bristol at twelve. Will set off from the said Tavern at Bristol at four o'clock every afternoon and arrive at London at eight o'clock the next morning. The price to and from Bristol, Bath and London, £1 8s. 0d. for each passenger. No outsides allowed. Both the Guards and Coachmen (who will likewise be armed) have given ample security for their conduct to the Proprietors so that those Ladies and Gentlemen who may please to honour them with their encouragement may depend on every respect and attention. Parcels will be forwarded agreeable to the direction immediately on their arrival at London, etc., and the price of porterage as well as the carriage on the most reasonable terms will be charged on the outside to prevent imposition. – Performed by Wilson & Co., London, Williams & Co., Bath. Note – The London, Bath and Bristol Coaches from above Inns as usual.'

It is sad that no first hand account of that first journey has survived, but there is no doubt about its success. The *Bath Chronicle* confirmed this in its issue dated 5 August 1784.

'The New Mail Diligence set off from Bristol on Monday last for the first time at four o'clock and from the Three Tunns in this City at twenty minutes after five the same evening. From London it set out at eight on Monday evening and was in Bath by nine the next morning. The excellent steps taken to carry on this undertaking leave not the least room to doubt its succeeding to the great pleasure and advantage of the Public. The Mail from this City is made up every evening at five o'clock.'

There was a further report in the issue for 12 August 1784.

'The New Mail Coach has travelled with an expedition that has been really astonishing, having seldom exceeded 13 hours in going to or returning from London. It is made very light, carries four passengers and runs with a pair of horses which are changed every six or eight miles, and as the bags at the different offices on the road are made up against its arrival there is not the least delay. The Guard rides with the Coachman on the Box and the Mail is deposited in the Boot. By this means the inhabitants of this City and Bristol have the London letters a day earlier than usual, a matter of great convenience to all and of much importance to merchants and tradesmen.'

The public, especially those engaged in any kind of business or commerce, were delighted, and it was certain before the end of the trial week that the mail coach would continue to run; and that the day of the postboy along the Bath Road, at least, was over. People whose affairs were less pressing and who lived away from the main road were perhaps not quite so enthusiastic, as the new service threw the bye- and cross-post services into confusion. Postboys' routes had often diverged from the main road in order to serve nearby towns and villages. Between Hungerford and Marlborough, for instance, they had gone by way of Ramsbury and Mildenhall. But such meanderings along unturnpiked roads were out of the question for fast coaches, and people living in those places found their letters delayed or left lying until collected at main road post offices. It was a long time before all the bye- and cross-posts were reorganised to fit in with the mail coach service. Postmasters, accustomed to the leisurely routines of the postboys, also found their lives disrupted, for the mail coach speeding through the night required them to rise from their beds twice in order

The original Bath Mail Coach

to receive, sort and forward the letters carried by the up and the down coach.

In the face of continued hostility, and even obstructive tactics, on the part of the Post Office, mail coaches were introduced by public demand in other parts of the country, and by 1787 they were running on all main routes in England and Scotland. Palmer, through Pitt's influence, was appointed Surveyor and Comptroller General of the Post Office in 1786, with a salary of £1,500 a year and special responsibility for the mail coach service. He remained in this post until his enemies contrived to get him dismissed in 1792.

One of his first concerns was the supply of suitable vehicles. The earliest coaches used were not up to the fast and sometimes furious speed at which they were driven, so that breakdowns were all too frequent. The coaches were supplied by the contractors who, it seems, thought that almost any vehicle would do for such rackety work, but Palmer was soon writing to inform them that the mails must be carried by more reliable coaches.

'The Comptroller General', he wrote to one contractor, 'has to complain not only of the quality of the horses employed on the Bristol Mail, but as well of their harness and the accoutrements in use, whose defects have several times delayed the Bath and Bristol and London letters, and have even led to the conveyance being overset, to the imminent peril of the passengers. Instructions have been issued by the Comptroller for new sets of harness to be supplied to the several coaches in use on this road, for which accounts will be sent you by the harness–makers. Mr Palmer has also under consideration, for the contractors' use, a new–invented coach.'

The new–invented coach was a 'patent coach' designed by John Besant, of Messrs Besant & Vidler of Millbank, a firm of coachbuilders which was to supply mail coaches for 40 years. Besant died in 1791, leaving John Vidler the sole owner until his death in 1826. Coaches were supplied to the contractors who paid a rental of 2½d. per double mile (that is a mile either way on a double journey). The coachbuilders serviced the vehicles regularly and kept them in repair for an additional fee, also chargeable to the contractors. Horses to draw the coach over their particular ground, as well as harness and coachmen were provided by the contractors at their expense; and they also paid a proportion of the bill for lamp oil.

Coaches of better design to that shown in the well-know print by Rowlandson of the first mail coach were introduced from time to time, an important change being made towards the end of the 18th century when the body of the coach and the coachman's box were combined into a single unit. This made life more comfortable for the coachman, who no longer sat on a springless box and boot fixed rigidly over the fore wheels while the body lurched and swung on independent supports behind him. It also made it possible for a seat for two outside passengers to be provided behind the coachman. One outside passenger had been allowed to sit beside the coachman (where the guard was not supposed to sit, having his own seat at the rear) since about 1791. The livery of the mail coaches never changed; from an early date the door and lower panels were maroon, the upper panels black, and the wheels red. On the doors were displayed the royal arms, and on the upper panels of the body the stars of the four orders of knighthood. On the side of the fore-boot was the cypher of the reigning monarch, and on the hind-boot the number of the coach. The words Royal Mail and the names of the two places at either end of the journey were lettered on the door and lower side panels. The standard of maintenance was very high. At the end of every return journey every coach was taken away to the Millbank works, cleaned, greased, overhauled and sent back in time for its next journey. Coaches which did not end their journeys in London were serviced elsewhere under special arrangements. After the trial runs, when the diligence had been drawn by only two horses, mail coaches along the Bath Road and all other long-distance routes were always drawn by four horses, except on the occasions when severe winter weather made extra horses necessary.

The coachmen who drove the early mails had learned their craft as stage coachmen. This meant that many had ingrained habits hard to break in the more exacting mail coach service, where time schedules were all-important. Rough, red-faced men, they had been encouraged in the habit of hard drinking by long hours of exposure to the weather and the succession of temptations placed in their way by inns and alehouses along the road. Although not often actually drunk in charge of the coach, they were reluctant to drive past the doors of friendly houses where they had been accustomed to drop in for something hot and strong to keep out the cold. Gradually these old-time coachmen, dressed in many-caped drab coats, thrashing and cursing their horses along the road in the effort to make up lost time, were replaced by a new generation of men trained in the mail-coach service. As roads became smoother, coaches better sprung, and stronger horses were bred for coach work, so did the coachmen take increasing pride in their job and their appearance. Neatly dressed in black beaver hats, smart box coats, cravats and often posies in their buttonholes, they were acknowledged experts in the art of driving, and the envy of every young blood whose ambition was to drive four-in-hand.

Whereas the coachman was employed by the contractors, who were responsible for the commercial operation of the service and received all the passenger fares, the guard was an employee of the Post Office, primarily responsible for the safety of the mails. In the event of a serious breakdown it was his duty to abandon the coach with its unlucky passengers, and taking one of the horses, to get the mailbags through as best he could on his own. Although guards were originally appointed to defend the mails from attacks by highwaymen, their mere presence acted as a powerful deterrent, and for many years few attacks took place. The worst perils encountered by guards in the course of their duty were those caused by severe winter weather, when many incidents were reported of guards struggling on through deep snow, icy floods and intense cold in order to carry the mails to the end of the journey as little behind time as possible.

Arduous though his work could be, and governed by strict rules and regulations at all times, there was generally a waiting list for a place as a guard. If selected, a candidate had to deposit £20 caution money, find two securities, take an oath of fidelity, and sign a lengthy sheet of instructions. His training began with two weeks at Vidler's coach-building establishment, where he was given a thorough grounding in the parts and functions of a coach and how to carry out roadside repairs. When he was ready for the road he was given his uniform, consisting of a tall black hat banded with gold braid and a scarlet coat cut in a military style and frogged with gold braid, as befitted a servant of the Royal Mail. He was also supplied with a blunderbuss, pistols and ammunition, a horn to give warning of the approach of the mail-coach, and a timepiece in a locked case. The guard was responsible for keeping the coach on time, and the timepiece was the mechanical means by which his masters at the Post Office kept a check on journey times in the days before Greenwich Mean Time, when local times could vary from place to place. The timepiece had to be handed over to the postmaster at certain stops and the time recorded on a time-bill, which had to be returned to the Post Office by the next up mail. There it was carefully scrutinised, and if any unaccounted-for delays were discovered, either the guard or the contractor, whichever was responsible, would receive a reprimand by the next post out of London.

The mail-bags were carried in a locked box built into the rear body of the coach, and the guard travelled with his feet resting on the box. Strict regulations forbade the mail-box to be unlocked at any time except for the stowage or removal of mail-bags, and failure to obey this rule was the cause of endless warning circulars sent to all guards similar to this one:–

'After this Notice, if ever you suffer your Mail-Box, when the Mail is therein, to remain unlocked, you will be forfeited a Week's Salary; – and if repeated, be dismissed from the Service. G.P.O. Aug 29. 1792.'

In May 1794 the guard of a Bristol-London mail got into hot water for leaving some of his mail-bags behind at Thatcham, where the Bristol and Bath and Exeter mails stopped regularly at the King's Head. While packing his sacks in the mail-box the guard was called away to attend to some other matter, with the result that the sack containing the bags from Chippenham, Calne, Marlborough, Hungerford and Newbury was left behind. The guard of the mail-coach going down to Bristol found the sack and took it to Newbury, the next post town, where he left it at the post office. Mr Barnes, the Postmaster, promptly hired a chaise and sent his assistant up to London with the sack, at the cost of five guineas. The unfortunate guard who had left the sack behind very nearly had to repay the whole of this sum, which amounted to ten weeks' pay, as a punishment, but having a good reputation as a sober and careful guard (usually), he was made to pay only half that amount.

The guard was in the tricky position of being responsible for the conduct of the coachman, and for reporting his misdemeanours and any accidents due to bad driving or negligence on the part of the contractors. Coachmen stopping at alehouses between stages under pretence of watering the horses was a fault which particularly roused the anger of Thomas Hasker, who succeeded Palmer with the title of Surveyor and Superintendent of the Mail-Coaches. Letters and circulars were sent to contractors and guards in a determined attempt 'to anihilate so shameful a Practice', and guards were warned, in peril of their situation, not to leave the coach nor to stop at any house except where there was lawful business to perform. If the coachman insisted on stopping, the guard must inform Hasker in writing. Nevertheless, the guard as well as the coachman sometimes succumbed to temptation, and in 1802 Hasker was disgusted to report that the horses drawing the Bristol Mail had bolted with the coach when left unattended outside the Magpies at Hounslow Heath.

Other circulars were issued warning guards not to linger at inns during bad weather, not to permit more than the lawful number of passengers to ride on the roof, not to carry any parcels on their own account, and not to use the mail-box for the carriage of fresh fish, poultry or game. The speed of the mail-coaches made them ideal vehicles for transporting fresh produce, and some guards were running profitable regular deliveries. A warning sent out in 1803 against carrying 'any Game, Fish, Fowl, Package or Parcels whatsoever clandestinely', contained the information that a warrant was out against a guard of the Bristol Mail (absconded) who had received stolen poultry.

From Hasker's correspondence can be told the sad tale of John Carter, who was the first guard of the Bristol to Bath and London mail-coach when it began to run in 1784. When he was given this post Carter, who lived near Marlborough, had already been in the post office service for nearly 30 years and had driven a mail cart on the Bristol road. After a few years as a guard Carter took to drinking heavily and, in 1794, Hasker was obliged to report to the Postmasters-General that he was no longer fit for service, 'having given himself up to drinking very much of late, which fault, on promises of great amendment being made, and in consideration of a good

Wife and many Children, he has several times been forgiven, but to no good purpose.' Lord Chesterfield, one of the Postmasters-General, recommended that Carter be given another chance, and as it was felt that he could no longer cope with the very fast changes necessary on the Bath and Bristol road, he was transferred to the Dover Foreign Mail, a quiet and unprofitable route at that time owing to the decline of communication with the Continent during the Napoleonic wars. Carter's case, however, was hopeless and when the Foreign Mail ceased to run altogether Hasker wrote again to the Postmasters-General submitting that, although Carter had been discharged at Marlborough for drunkenness, he had served the Post Office for nearly 40 years and in consideration of this, and the extreme distress of his wife and eight children, he should be allowed the pension given to superannuated guards.

Their Lordships replied, 'Certainly.'

West of England mails preparing to start from the Swan with Two Necks, Lad Lane

Like the coachman, the mail-guard enjoyed considerable prestige. On the road his coach took precedence over other traffic, so that, at a blast from his horn, all vehicles were obliged to draw aside to make way for the mail. At turnpike gates the Royal Mail paid no toll, and the sound of the guard's horn was the signal for the pike-keeper to be ready with his gate open so that the mail could go through at top speed. At times like these the guard, in his scarlet and gold uniform, must have looked and felt a splendid fellow.

Mail coaches left London for all parts of England every night at 8 o'clock. The coaches were timed to depart from the City inns, with their passengers on board, at 7.30, and from there they made their way to the General Post Office in Lombard Street where the mailbags were loaded into the boxes. If, as sometimes happened, the Post Office was late with the mail, or loading took longer than usual, the passengers could grow impatient and wander off to nearby coffee houses, where they had to be looked for when the coach was ready to start. The Bath coaches for many years began their journey at the Swan with Two Necks in Lad Lane but by the 1820s Lombard Street had become so congested that all the West Country mail coaches went direct to the Gloucester Coffee House in Piccadilly, where they waited for the guards to bring the mailbags which they had collected from the G.P.O. in small mail carts. This arrangement both saved time and lessened the inconvenience for passengers. The Gloucester Coffee House must also have found the arrangement very satisfactory. At 8 o'clock the West Country mails moved off in what must have been a magnificent procession, bound for Bath, Bristol, Portsmouth, Exeter, Southampton, Devonport, Poole and Gloucester, and all followed the Bath Road as far as Hounslow or Maidenhead.

Once the timetable for the Bath and Bristol mails had been established it varied very little, and the journey time was hardly reduced until the 1820s. According to the passenger timetable printed in Cary's *New Itinerary* for 1806 and 1817 the Bath coach was due to arrive at towns along the route at the following times:– Brentford 9.20 p.m., Hounslow 9.40, Colnbrook 10.35, Slough 11.05, Maidenhead 11.45, Reading 1.25 a.m., Newbury 3.30, Hungerford 4.40, Marlborough 6.00, Calne 7.20, Chippenham 8.00, and Bath 9.30 a.m.

The up mail left Bath at 5.30 p.m. and reached Chippenham at 7.05, Calne 8.00, Marlborough 9.30, Hungerford 10.40, Newbury 11.35, Reading 1.55 a.m., Maidenhead 3.30, Slough 4.15, Colnbrook 4.45, Hounslow 5.30, Brentford 5.45 and London around 7.00 a.m.

The coach stopped at other places, not mentioned by Cary, to change horses and to receive and deliver mail bags. At Thatcham a twenty minute break was allowed at the King's Head for refreshments, the down coach being due to arrive there at 2.45 and to be off again at 3.05 a.m. The up and down coaches must have met somewhere on the road between Reading and Newbury.

It was only rarely that these timetables were thrown into confusion, but, then as now, snow could cause chaos overnight. In February 1799 all the mails were delayed by a heavy fall of snow, many coaches being stuck fast in snowdrifts. Owing, it was said, to improvements on the Bath Road it proved possible for the Bath and Exeter mails to be pulled through by teams of six horses, so that they arrived only about three hours later than usual. Conditions were much worse in February 1808 when a snowstorm beginning on the night of Thursday 18th was so severe that only half the 20 mails due in London early on Saturday morning had arrived by 1 p.m. Distressing reports were brought in from all over the country of travellers frozen to death or killed when coaches overturned. On several routes, where guards attempted to carry the mailbags forward on horseback, the horses were killed by falls or died from cold and exhaustion. On the Bath Road, as the London to Exeter mail-coach was going down Marlborough Hill on the Thursday night, the horses sank into a snowdrift and, before they could be dug out, two of them had died.

The most famous snowstorm in coaching history was

Mail coach stranded in a snowdrift. The guard, mounted on one of the leaders, can be seen riding on ahead with the mail-bags

that which took place at Christmas 1836. Snow began to fall in the north on Christmas Eve and during the night a thick blanket spread southwards over the whole country. It was a white Christmas with a vengeance. On Christmas morning only a handful of coaches had arrived in London by 8.30, although a few others straggled in later in the day. By the morning of Boxing Day the situation had worsened. Not one of the night mails had arrived. The Poole, Portsmouth and Ipswich mails reached London by midday, but the Dover, Hastings, Brighton, Chester, Edinburgh, Liverpool and Leeds mails were still missing. On roads all over the country coachmen and horses struggled valiantly to get the mail-coaches through, but in many places the line of the road was invisible and the coachmen were driving in the teeth of a bitter wind and blinded by swirling snow. Some who got down from their boxes to assist the horses were immediately buried in snowdrifts, and were lucky if they and their coaches were dug out and hauled to safety by farm horses. Fourteen mail-coaches were abandoned on various roads and others were forced to turn back without completing their journeys.

Over the Wiltshire Downs the roads were reported to be dreadful, with snowdrifts 12-16 feet deep between Marlborough and Devizes. The Bath and Bristol mails which set out on Monday night (26 December) had to be abandoned 80 miles from London. The two guards brought the mailbags on in a postchaise drawn by four horses, and reached London at 6 o'clock on Wednesday morning. They reported that for 17 miles of the way they had driven across fields.

The Duke of Wellington, who set out on Boxing Day in his carriage and four with outriders to visit the Duke of Beaufort at Badminton, was obliged to spend the night at the Castle Inn at Marlborough. The next morning he set out again, but his carriage got stuck in the snow in a wheatfield. Fortunately a road surveyor who was working not far away came to his assistance, and the Duke's carriage was dug out by labourers and piloted across country until it reached a sound-bottomed road. The drifts near Marlborough were so deep that gangs of labourers were employed to clear the snow from the Bath Road for a distance of four miles.

That same Christmas, three outside passengers on a stage coach had died of cold by the time the coach reached Chippenham; and in the days that followed reports of many other tragedies poured in from all over the country.

8

Inns and Innkeeping

The famous inn at Speenhamland
That stands below the hill,
May well be called the Pelican
From its enormous bill.

These well-known lines have been attributed to the 18th century actor, James Quin, and if they were truly his it is very likely that the bill presented to him was, indeed, enormous. For Quin was famous for his gargantuan capacity for good food and wine. A man of huge girth, his most successful part on stage was that of Falstaff. Off stage he was a great talker, a great wit and a favourite guest of Ralph Allen at Prior Park. When he retired from the stage in 1751 Quin went to live in Bath, and he is buried there in the Abbey.

The full name of the inn where he is said to have scratched these lines on a window pane was the George and Pelican. It was one of a cluster of inns at Speenhamland, the northern part of the town of Newbury, which developed to serve the traffic along the Bath Road. Roughly halfway between London and Bath, it was a convenient place for breaking the journey overnight, and Quin was only one of many notable people who stayed there. Royalty, statesmen, generals, admirals (including Nelson) and eminent divines all patronised the Pelican. It was recognised as one of the best-conducted inns on the Bath Road, and its prices were accordingly high. Other inns at Speenhamland were the Chequers, the Bear, the Bacon Arms, the Lamb and Flag, the King's Arms, the humbler Cross Keys where stage-coach passengers often stopped for supper, and in a quieter situation on the hill above Speenhamland the

> CASTLE INN, SPEEN-HILL,
> Near NEWBURY.
>
> TO be LETT or SOLD, and entered on imme-
> diately,——The above mentioned CAPITAL INN,
> pleafantly fituated on the Great Bath Road, in the midway
> between London and Bath, commanding a delightful prof-
> pect, and confifting of every convenience and accommodation
> for travellers of the firft rank, having been occupied by Mr.
> SMITH, the tenant lately deceafed, for near thirty years paft,
> and continued to the prefent time in full trade.
>
> The apartments are exceedingly commodious, the cellars
> good, and the ftables and offices in every refpect well adapted
> to the trade of a capital inn There are about eight acres of
> good pafture land belonging to the premifes.
>
> For particulars, enquire of Mr. Thomas Halliwell, or Mr.
> Townfend, Attorney, at Newbury; Meffrs. Berkley and
> Burgh, Garden Court, Temple, London; Mr. Wickens. at
> Sulhampftead, near Reading, or Mr. John Watts, at That-
> cham, near Newbury.

The Castle Inn, on Speen Hill, for sale, 1786

Castle Inn, which like the Pelican was sometimes patronised by royalty.

Wherever the Bath Road ran through a town or village, inns flourished. Colnbrook, Maidenhead, Reading, Marlborough and Chippenham also boasted important inns as well as a variety of lesser ones, and in many smaller places inns were the most prominent buildings. A revised edition of Defoe's *Tour*, published in 1748, had little to say about Thatcham, Woolhampton, Theale and Twyford except that they were full of inns. Slough was said to consist almost entirely of inns, 'they seem to vie with one another, and 'tis wonderful how they all subsist; especially as they are opposed by the two famous new ones of the Castle and Windmill, a little way out of Slough, which are much more delightfully situated, and have better Accommodations.'

The inns and the road were mutually dependent. While the inns thrived on the custom brought by the travellers, the road, no matter how much improved, could not have carried such a volume of traffic without the services provided by inns. They were essential to the traveller and to his horses. In an age when an average speed of six or seven miles an hour was considered good progress, stops were needed every ten or so miles to bait or change horses; while the traveller himself required rest, refreshment, a bed for the night, security from nocturnal attacks by robbers, and sometimes shelter from the weather. Neither stage nor mail coach services could have developed so easily without the facilities provided by inns, and as travel speeded up towards the end of the 18th century the supply and stabling of horses became almost more important than services to humans. 'Most inns now', wrote the Hon. John Byng in 1790, are kept by, and for a change of post horses, as fine gentlemen never step out of their chaises on the longest journeys; and all others travel in the mail, or post coaches: so that the tourist who only wants a supper, and a bed, is consider'd as a troublesome unprofitable intruder.'

At the height of the coaching era the larger inns were centres of ceaseless and varied activity. Behind the imposing fronts presented to the street those with room to expand grew into huge, rambling complexes. An archway, high enough to allow laden coaches to enter, gave access to a yard at the rear around which were picturesque and often ancient wings consisting, at ground level, of stables, and on the upper floors of bedrooms opening onto galleries overlooking the yard. Along one side of the yard there was often a paved and covered way leading travellers who had just descended from their coaches to the reception hall, coffee rooms and dining parlours. Some inns had separate dining parlours for public coach passengers, thus segregating those unlucky people, who were hardly allowed sufficient time to eat or drink before being hustled back onto their coach, from the wealthier travellers who had leisure to enjoy a good meal.

On the opposite side of the yard from the reception rooms the booking office could usually be found. This

Stage-coach arriving at an inn, from a print by Pollard, 1816

was very likely the one used for post office business in the days when innkeepers were postmasters, but as pressure of business moved post offices out into separate premises, the office at the inn came to be used for booking seats on coaches and arranging other matters, such as the despatch of parcels and the hire of post-chaises and postilions.

Coaching inns gave employment to a great many people and relied upon the services of a variety of local tradesmen and craftsmen. Chambermaids, barmaids, cooks, waiters and bootboys attended to the travellers; while ostlers, grooms and stable-lads took care of the horses. Smiths and farriers might also be called upon to attend to the horses; and blacksmiths, wheelwrights and harness-makers to deal with breakdowns. Food, wine, straw and provender had to be ordered in quantities, and the clerical work of the booking office had also to be attended to.

In addition to their many services to travellers, inns were centres of local social life. Some of the larger ones boasted assembly rooms, where balls and card parties could be held. Nearly all of them had private rooms for hire for dinners and meetings of a convivial or official nature. Inn yards were no longer used for the performance of plays by troupes of strolling players but inns retained a link with the theatre by acting as booking offices. In the late 18th century theatres were opened in many provincial towns, and particularly in those where there were plenty of wealthy travellers as well as local gentry to support them. On the Bath Road a small theatre was fitted up at the Marquis of Granby, (formerly the Gallows Tavern) on the outskirts of Reading, in 1786, but this failed to prosper and two years later another theatre was opened in the centre of the town. There was already a theatre at Newbury which, like that at Reading, belonged to Henry Thornton, an enterprising theatre manager with a growing circuit in the south of England. Both flourished for many years. The Reading theatre was rebuilt in a more elaborate style in 1801, and a new theatre was built at Speenhamland, very convenient for the inns, in 1802. Leading stars of the London stage, the Kembles, Dorothy Jordan and others, performed with Thornton's regular company.

Theatre seasons were short, rarely amounting to more than a few weeks once or twice a year, but they were invariably open while local race meetings were being held. These attracted a great many sporting gentlemen and other visitors to the neighbourhood. Most coaching inns then sold theatre tickets, and at certain of them horses could be entered for the races. Entrance fees for each horse were usually one guinea and owners were expected to subscribe two or more guineas towards the prize plate or purse. In the late 18th century race meetings were held at Maidenhead, near the Thicket, at Reading on Bulmershe Heath, at Newbury on Wash Common, and at Marlborough on Barton Down. The meetings were great social events involving many leading townspeople. The *Marlborough Journal*, advertising a race meeting in 1771, announced a race on the first day for the Noblemen and Gentlemen's Subscription Plate of £50, and on the second day for the Town Plate of £50. All disputes were to be settled by the Mayor. An ordinary (a meal at a fixed price) was provided at the Castle Inn on the first day and at the White Hart on the second. In the evening there was an assembly at the White Hart, and to accommodate the ladies and gentlemen a coach was kept in readiness to set them down after the ball at any house in the town, gratis.

Bowling and cock fighting were other sports catered for by inns. The Pelican at Speenhamland, the King's Arms and the Crown at Reading, all had bowling greens where gentlemen could while away a pleasant hour or two. The Bear at Speenhamland was noted for its cockpit and some of the most famous battles in the history of this once-popular sport took place there. Cockfights were held in most other towns along the Bath Road. A typical notice in the *Reading Mercury* in 1770 informed those interested that 'A Main of cocks will be shewn at the Cross Keys in Reading on 27 August and fought on the following 3 days, being the time of the races, between the Gentlemen of Berkshire and Oxfordshire. 31 Cocks in the Main, for 4 guineas a Battle, and forty the odd Battle, and fifteen to the Byes for 2 guineas a battle.'

Bath Road inns catered for travellers of every rank and kind. They ranged from the Castle at Marlborough, originally a nobleman's house and converted after 1752 into one of the grandest and most fashionable inns in England, to the unassuming Quart Pot where wagoners slaked their thirst at Maidenhead. There were inns whose recurrent medieval names bore witness to their long-established worth; the Bear at Maidenhead, Reading, Hungerford, Devizes and Sandy Lane; the Crown at Slough, Reading, Theale and Thatcham; the Angel at Woolhampton and Chippenham. There were inns with shady reputations, such as the Halfway House, less than a mile from Hyde Park Corner, where it was said that highwaymen's touts gathered to collect information on wealthy people setting out on journeys down the Bath Road. Other inns rose in the world during the prosperous coaching age and changed their names to the more aristocratic ones of local landowners. Such were the Lansdowne Arms, formerly the Catherine Wheel, at Calne, and the Methuen Arms, formerly the Red Lion, at Corsham. In country areas smaller inns had names appropriate to the modest wayfarers who frequented them, such as the Old Pack Horse at Turnham Green, the Horse and Groom at Hare Hatch, the Rising Sun at Beenham, and the Wagon and Horses at Twyford, Beckhampton and elsewhere.

Innkeepers often had to cope with travellers in a poor state of health, either on their way to seek a cure or returning home, and sometimes too ill to undertake the journey. In 1767 the Earl of Chatham, on his way home from Bath, was confined for some weeks with an attack of gout at the Castle Inn at Marlborough. The inn, which had been a private residence only a few years previously, almost became one again, for the Earl insisted that all the inn servants should wear his livery throughout his stay. In October 1784 the Earl Waldegrave, General of His Majesty's Forces, died on his way to Bath, where he was going for the recovery of his health. He spent his last

The inn yard at the White Hart in Calne

night at the Crown Inn at Reading, and next morning was taken so ill in his carriage with what was believed to be a fit of apoplexy that he was forced to stop at Theale, where he died. In January 1806 William Pitt, by then a very sick man, travelled back from a month's stay in Bath by easy stages, taking three days over the journey. On the night of the 10th he stayed at the Crown in Reading, where the local newspaper reported that his medical advisers were not without hope that he might be able to resume his official duties. But this was not to be. On the 11th he moved slowly on to Salt Hill, where he stayed at the Windmill, before completing his journey to London. He died at his home in Putney on 23 January.

In the days when kings and queens put up at inns and only the poorest of their subjects could not find one to accommodate them, there must have been few people so determined as John Elwes, M.P., to avoid putting money into the pockets of innkeepers. Although possessed of a large fortune, he arranged matters so that a journey from London to his estate in Berkshire should cost him no more than fourpence. His biographer relates, 'Had every man been of the mind of Mr Elwes, the race of innkeepers must have perished, and post chaises have been returned back to those who made them; for it was the business of his life to avoid both. He always travelled on horseback. To see him setting out on a journey, was a matter truly curious; his first care was to put two or three eggs, boiled hard, into his great coat pocket, or any scraps of bread which he found – baggage he never took – then, mounting one of his hunters, his next attention was to get out of London, into that road where the turnpikes were fewest. Then, stopping under any hedge where grass presented itself for his horse, and a little water for himself, he would sit down and refresh himself and his horse together.'

A very different kind of traveller was the Hon. John Byng, who inherited the title of Viscount Torrington shortly before his death, and who undertook many journeys for pleasure in the 1780s and 90s. Byng confessed himself old-fashioned in his tastes and habits, and looked back nostalgically to the roads and inns and customs of his youth. Not for him was the shabby, hurrying post-chaise or the stuffy, crowded coach. When he went on one of his summer tours he rode at a leisurely pace on what he called 'a sufficient horse', carrying a small portmanteau behind him. Of his horse he took great care, and he made a point of inspecting the stables wherever he stopped for the night; 'for', he wrote, 'if my horse does not fare and sleep well, why there would be an end of my travel.'

A servant usually rode on ahead of him to carry the bulk of his luggage and make sure that proper accommodation was ready at the inn where he planned to spend the night. 'This is the true use of servants on the road, tho' but seldom what their masters require of them; trusting to the waiter, and chambermaid for dirty glasses, and ill-made beds, and confiding the care of their horses to drunken, roguish hostlers; and whilst their own genteel followers are regaling themselves in a genteel parlour, the horses are neither clean'd nor fed. As for my sheets I always take them with me, knowing that next to a certainty, 5 sheets must be dirty, and 3 damp, out of number 10; these with a very few other necessaries, travell behind my servant; as for my night cap, great coat, and such other etceteras, they travell behind my own person, in and upon a small cloakbag.'

The other etceteras included a supply of James's powders, in case he fell ill of a fever and did not wish to consult 'the medical country blockheads', a collection of maps and road books, because inn servants could never direct him along the right road, and a large bundle of newspapers with which he whiled away the time beween supper and bed in places where no other amusements, such as theatrical performances, of which he was very fond, were offered. The bundle of newspapers must have been quite a prominent piece of luggage, for on one occasion when he was setting out on a tour, the pike-keeper at Hyde Park turnpike enquired whether he would like some more newspapers for his cargo. Byng was not sure whether this was intended as wit or civility.

In the mornings he liked to make an early start. 'I call for the bill in the night before my departure; rise early; eat a slice of bread and butter, and drink some milk, that I took upstairs with me; then ride ten miles to breakfast; there shirt and shave; by which means I get a forward day; and my horse baits while I dress; whereas by waiting (at the bed-inn) for a barber, and a breakfast, the finest hours in fine weather are lost; and the delay may lead to a dark evening ride.'

Byng hated the new turnpike roads, which he considered ugly, flat and straight, although there were times when he was glad to make use of them. He complained that they brought a sameness of manners, speech and customs into every district, and wrote, in one of his more peevish moods, 'I wish with all my heart that half the turnpike roads of the kingdom were plough'd up, which have imported London manners, and depopulated the country – I meet milkmaids on the road, with the dress and looks of Strand misses; and must think that every line of Goldsmith's Deserted Village contains melancholy truths.'

Town inns he condemned as dismal, noisy places, many of them awkwardly situated in dark, narrow streets, and having cramped and dirty stables. The Bear at Reading (one of the two best inns in the town) did not come up to his exacting standards. On one occasion his evening bowl of punch was sour and weak, and when he retired to bed he suspected that the sheets were damp, so that, apparently being without his own, he had to sleep in the blankets. On another visit the Bear Inn was so crowded that he had to share a room, and his horses one stall between them. 'An impertinent, hurrying inn', he called it, and only so busy because the King's Arms further along the Bath Road was closed.

He liked best a quiet, well-conducted inn, with attentive servants and good food and wine. He commended as 'one of the best inns I know' the Windmill at Salt Hill, run by the elderly Mr and Mrs March. It was there that he recorded an amusing incident involving Mr March and a mourning coach. It was the landlord's custom to hobble out to welcome new arrivals, attended by a waiter bearing a tray of cakes and other small refreshments. One day a black coach drew up with what appeared to be mourners seated inside, whom Mr March greeted with his usual 'What do you choose, gem'mem; biscuits, cakes, jellies?' There was no answer, and the kind old man had turned to the waiter to say that the gentlemen were so oppressed with grief that they did not want anything, when a post-horse put its head through the coach window and 'tore out of the bowells of one of these gentlemen', who in truth were nothing but mourning cloaks stuffed with straw.

A short distance to the west of the Windmill, and on the south side of the Bath Road at Salt-hill, there was another famous inn called the Castle, so named because of the fine view it commanded of Windsor Castle. Both these inns were associated with the Eton Montem ceremony which gave Salt-hill its name. Dating back to the 16th century, this had begun as an annual event but, from 1775, it was held triennially. On Whit-Tuesday the younger boys of Eton College set off before six in the morning to collect money, or 'salt' as they called it, from travellers along the road between Colnbrook and Maidenhead. The boys much enjoyed playing at highwaymen and not even members of the royal family were allowed to pass without contributing. Meanwhile a house to house collection was carried out in Eton and, at the College, an impressive ceremony was staged in the quadrangle by the senior boys and staff, dressed in elaborate costumes and watched by crowds of visitors. After the ceremony they proceeded *ad montem*, that is, towards a small grassy mound beside the Bath Road where it is joined by the road from Eton, and where the younger boys were also gathered. Some prayers were said in latin, a flag was unfurled upon the mound, and the whole company ended the day with a rousing banquet at the Castle or the Windmill Inn. The money collected during the day often amounted to several hundred pounds and was intended to help pay for the university education of the Captain of Montem, the highest Colleger in the school, but some of it went towards the Montem expenses, the costumes, the band and the wine and food at the banquet. The Eton Montem was a popular event in the 18th century but became too extravagant and riotous to suit the more sober tastes of the 19th century, and it was held for the last time in 1844.

By that time the Castle Inn was closed and had become a private house. Many years before its reputation had been severely damaged by a poisoning scandal, from which it never completely recovered. The Castle and the Windmill were among the excellent inns, where a good dinner could be relied upon, which were used by the Colnbrook Turnpike Trustees for their meetings, and it was at the Castle that they met on the fatal 29 March 1773.

Those present were the Hon. Mr Needham, Captain O'Brien, Major Mayne, Edward Mason, Esq., Mr Cheshire, Walpole Eyre, Esq., Captain Salter, Mr Isherwood, Mr Benwell the Treasurer, Mr Burcombe the Surveyor, and Mr Pote, a printer from Eton. The business of the day evidently included some magisterial duties as well as matters concerning the turnpike trust, for during the morning they examined some paupers due to be returned to their own parishes. One of them was said to be in a particularly weak and wretched condition. Having decided the immediate future of these unfortunate people the gentlemen sat down to dine, the meal spread before them consisting of turtle soup; fish, jack, perch and eel spitch-cockt; fowls, bacon and greens; veal cutlets, ragout of pigs' ears, chine of mutton and salad; course of lamb and cucumbers; crayfish; pastry and jellies. The dinner, so the newspapers asserted when the affair was brought to light, 'was plain and innocent, nothing high-seasoned, or that could give cause of suspicion of any bad consequence; the wine, madeira and port of the best sorts. In both articles of meat and drink, the company were moderate and no excess appeared.'

All was not so plain and innocent as it seemed. Within a short time (first reports were reluctant to admit how short) nearly all those present were taken ill, and Mr Needham, Mr Eyre, Mr Isherwood, Mr Benwell and Mr

Burcombe died. Captain Salter, Mr Mason and Mr Cheshire were all violently sick but recovered; Captain O'Brien was dangerously ill for some time, and Major Mayne's life was so despaired of that he was at one time reported dead.

Suspicion fell immediately upon the food and wine consumed at the dinner. Rumours began to fly and the reputation of the Castle Inn was in a fair way to being ruined. The landlady, Mrs Partridge, vehemently denied that anything eaten or drunk in her house could possibly be at fault, and made it known that her kitchen, cellar and every article connected with the dinner had been thoroughly inspected and declared free from blame. The alternative explanation put forward was that the wretched pauper who had been examined just before the dinner had been suffering from some contagious disease. His deplorable condition was dwelt upon and it was suggested that he had gaol fever. The following arguments were put forward in support of this theory:–

i) Mr Pote the printer, who was not a trustee, had only attended the meeting on business and had left the room to walk in the garden while the examination of the paupers took place. He alone had suffered no ill effects, and yet he had dined afterwards at the same table and had drunk the same wines as the other gentlemen.

ii) Dr James, the physician attending Major Mayne, gave it as his opinion that the disease of which the others had died was caught by infection and was not caused by anything eaten or drunk. The first symptoms, he said, had not appeared until eleven days after the meeting, whereas anything of a poisonous nature always operated within hours of its being taken.

iii) Mr Burcombe the Surveyor, who had been present during the examination of the paupers, and who had died, did not dine with the others but ate beef-steaks for his dinner in a private room below stairs.

iv) The gentlemen had drunk only the same wine which they had commended at a previous meeting, and which many other people had drunk before and since.

Another report, hardly credible, said that on the day of the meeting some felons had been moved from Reading Gaol to London, on their way to be transported, and had stopped at the Castle while the meeting was in progress. This was only one of the many stories which spread all over the countryside and up to London when news of the dreadful event leaked out. At the end of April it was all over town, being reported in full in the *Gazetteer, Lloyd's Evening Post*, and other London newspapers. Also printed were letters from several other medical men supporting Dr James' opinion that the sickness was due to fever and not to poison. It says much for the high standing of the Castle Inn and the reputation of its landlady that so many people were prepared to speak out to defend her. Mr Pote even went to the lengths of printing and distributing handbills all over Windsor and district declaring that a contagious distemper had been brought by vagabonds to Mrs Partridge's and that the fact that the symptoms had not appeared until eleven days after the meeting proved that this was the true explanation.

Mr Pote's action, however well meant, spread alarm among the inhabitants of Windsor, and a counter attack was launched in a letter published in the *Gazetteer* of 30 April, signed 'A Well-wisher to the Public'. Well-wisher claimed that the story of a contagious fever had been spread for their own private ends by persons who had not scrupled to terrify the public, to the particular detriment of the town of Windsor. The statement that the symptoms did not appear for eleven days was quite untrue, for it was well-known that Mr Isherwood's life had been despaired of before then and that, in fact, the whole company had been taken ill on the very night following the dinner, whatever Dr James, or anyone else, might say. The argument that Mr Burcombe had eaten beef-steaks on his own below stairs was no proof that the wine which he had drunk above stairs had not been the cause of his death. If the sickness had really been caught from the poor wretches brought before the magistrates, why had no one else at the inn been infected? Why had not Mrs Partridge endeavoured to trace the pauper to find out whether he really was ill? Why had none of those who had attended the sick gentlemen caught the infection? Dr James had tried to save the reputation of Mrs Partridge's house by injudiciously opposing his reasoning to known facts; and all for what? For supporting an individual at the expense of the quiet of the country; by this means setting a mark upon Windsor as an infected place, deterring strangers and injuring the inhabitants, when at this time there was no more wholesome spot in Europe. It was generally believed that the wine was tainted, and although Mrs Partridge was to be pitied, it was better that the public should know this than that they should be alarmed by rumours of contagion.

Mrs Partridge stuck to her story and replied, through the columns of the same newspaper, that the pauper had indeed been traced. The poor fellow, who was now named as James Jackson, was found ill of a fever in the stables of a Mr March at Taplow. He had been nursed by a Mrs Matthews, who was taken ill with the same fever and recovered, but her husband had died of it. The Rev. Mr Hamilton of Taplow would confirm this. On 29 March, the day of the meeting, Jackson had been brought in a cart by the parish officer to the Castle Inn, where the gentlemen had given orders that he should be moved to Wooburn, and there he had been taken in a cart and deposited in an outhouse belonging to the Royal Oak. A woman who looked after him there was stricken within 10 or 12 days with the fever and died; and the barber who shaved him had been taken seriously ill.

This sad story was refuted two or three weeks later by a correspondent who stated that the poor man had not been weak from fever but from starvation; that the woman who took care of him at Taplow was very well and that her husband who died had been ill for nine years. The woman who died at Wooburn was very old and ill before Jackson was brought there; none of Mr March's family or servants who had visited him in his distress had been taken ill, and there was no malignant fever in the country.

A correspondent describing himself as 'A Friend to the Indigent Poor' expressed the opinion that the deaths of the trustees had been caused by wine refined with arsenic, and this, or some other 'pernicious ingredient' used in refining wine, was widely believed to have been the cause of the tragedy.

There, for many years, the matter rested. The Castle Inn lost a good deal of business but it survived with the support of Mrs Partridge's many friends. When the Eton Montem was held on Whit-Tuesday that year, the dinner was held at the Windmill and none of the boys were allowed to go to the Castle, but this did not prevent many visitors to the ceremony from favouring Mrs Partridge with their custom. The Colnbrook Trustees continued to hold meetings at the Castle alternately with the Windmill as before, and no reference was made in their minutes to the manner of their colleagues' deaths. In June 1773 they advertised for a new Treasurer 'in the room of the late Joseph Benwell decd.' and a Surveyor 'in the room of the late William Burcombe deceased.' They also ordered that no business should be transacted at any future meeting in the room where they met but such as concerned the turnpike road only. In July they set about appointing some new trustees 'in the room of some deceased.'

The clerk who made the entries in the parish register at Burnham was less discreet, and recorded the burial on 26 April of 'Walpole Eyre, East Burnham, aged 38, died April 18; one of those unfortunate gentlemen who dined at ye Castle Inn 29 March.'

The truth leaked out many years later and was revealed in the Memoirs of Mrs Charlotte Papendiek, Assistant Keeper of the Wardrobe to Queen Charlotte, who lived at Windsor. She had heard that, on her deathbed, Mrs Partridge had confessed her guilty secret; that the turtle soup had been left standing overnight in a copper pan and reheated on the following morning, by which time the bottom was green with verdigris. It was of this poison, caused by the action of acid flavourings on the copper, that the unfortunate gentlemen had died. It had been an accident; the cook had not known of the danger. As for

Mr Burcombe the Surveyor, who was supposed to have eaten beefsteaks in a room below stairs, he had in fact dined freely on the remains of the dishes as they were brought out from the dining room.

9

Highway Robbery

Let us take the road!
Hark! I hear the sound of coaches,
The hour of attack approaches,
To your arms, brave boys, and load!
John Gay: *The Beggar's Opera.* 1728.

On Hounslow Heath, where the roads from Bath and
Exeter meet, there stood for a century or more a row of
gibbets on which the bodies of highwaymen and other
malefactors were hung in irons after execution. Placed as
they were within sight of two of the busiest roads into
London, and laden as often as not with grisly burdens, the
gibbets became a familiar landmark for travellers and a
popular attraction for sightseers with a taste for such
things.

According to a mid-18th century survey, Hounslow
Heath extended over more than 6,000 acres of south-west
Middlesex, and until the end of that century much of it
was an empty waste, useless alike for arable farming or
pasture. The few 'greyhound-like' sheep which grazed
there were 'pitiful, half-starved looking animals, subject
to rot'. From earliest times man had found little use for
the Heath except as a place for hunting and hawking,
military encampments and exercises, and the
manufacture of explosive substances. Gunpowder mills
were established near Hounslow early in the 17th century
and survived into the 20th, their history being punctuated
by explosions occurring at various dates up to 1915. None
of these activities, however, was responsible for the
Heath's dangerous reputation. That was due entirely to
the highwaymen who roamed the area.

In the coaching age there was hardly a road out of

London which did not pass over some wild common or wooded tract of country where highwaymen and footpads lay in wait. Finchley Common, on the Great North Road, was equally notorious; and other dangerous places were Watford Gap, Shooters Hill, Blackheath, Kennington and Putney Commons. Along the roads to all these places laden gibbets announced to travellers that justice had been done on at least a tiny proportion of the robbers who infested the roads, but the knowledge was small comfort to them. Hanging and gibbetting appeared in no way to discourage the others, and the numbers of robberies continued to increase alarmingly.

Hounslow Heath was particularly favoured by highwaymen because the Exeter Road via Staines crossed it and the Bath and Bristol Road ran along its northern edge; and both were capable of yielding a rich booty from the wealthy travellers who passed along them. The Bath Road near London was exceedingly profitable, for it was used not only by people going to Bath and other west of England towns and country seats, but by the royal family and nobility going to the Court at Windsor. Dukes, Earls, bishops and highborn, bejewelled ladies were common prey for the highwaymen of Hounslow Heath, who became so bold and confident that even the King was not considered safe from their attentions, and in the 18th century a horse patrol was stationed at Gunnersbury to guard His Majesty's coach on the way to Windsor. It was fortunate that not all highwaymen were the worst of blackguards, for one day in 1741 one of them held up a coach containing three small children and a nursemaid. 'Who are these pretty dears?', demanded the highwayman. 'The grandchildren of your King', replied the terrified nursemaid. 'God bless His Majesty', said the highwayman, and let the coach pass.

Even after crossing the Heath the London-bound traveller was not out of danger, for the road between the village of Kensington and Knightsbridge had as bad a reputation for robberies as it had for the depths of its mud. John Evelyn noted the prevalence of robberies here in the middle of the 17th century, and the sad fate of one man was recorded in the burial registers of St Mary Abbot's, Kensington, when Thomas Ridge of Portsmouth was 'killed by thieves almost at Knightsbridge'. Another typical incident was described in the *Gentleman's Magazine* of April 1740, when the Bristol Mail from London was robbed a little beyond Knightsbridge by a man on foot, who took the Bath and Bristol bags, and mounting the postboy's horse, rode off towards London.

Between Kensington and Knightsbridge stood the Halfway House, an inn known to be a meeting-place for robbers in search of useful information. In 1752 a professional thief-taker named Norton was instructed to go to Knightsbridge to try to catch a highwayman who had several times robbed the Devizes coach. Norton was driven in a chaise towards the inn, and as he drew near, the driver was stopped and threatened by a man with a pistol. Norton leaped down from the chaise and after a struggle arrested the man, a certain William Belchier, who was later hanged. It was incidents such as these which led to the custom of ringing a bell at Kensington on Sunday evenings to summon people returning to London into groups for safety.

London itself was the most dangerous place of all. People were robbed in broad daylight in the most fashionable parts of town, so that swords, pistols and even blunderbusses were carried on the shortest journeys, and Horace Walpole complained that 'one is forced to travel, even at noon, as if one was going into battle.' Henry Fielding, London's overworked chief magistrate, remarked in his *Enquiry into the Causes of the Late Increase of Robbers* in 1751 that 'the streets of this town, and the roads leading into it, will shortly be impassable without the utmost hazard'. He, and his brother John, who succeeded him at Bow Street, recognised that the seething, overcrowded cities of London and Westminster, with their appalling slums, were breeding grounds for vice and crime. Thieves could harbour there in safety, and 'fences' were so numerous that they had no difficulty at all in disposing of stolen goods. The Fieldings strove to promote the idea of a strong and unified police force to combat crime but the resources available to them were too small and the task too huge for them to make much headway.

Criminals were not only too numerous and well-organised, but certain of them were popular heroes. Many a highwayman, bravely swaggering to the end, was hanged at Tyburn surrounded by crowds of admiring, grieving onlookers. When John Gay created the immortal figure of Captain Macheath he must certainly have hoped that his *Beggar's Opera* would take the public fancy but he can hardly have guessed that it would become the rage of town, and be revived again and again, there and in the provinces, until the end of the century. In the eyes of moralists its delightful airs in no way compensated for the corruptive influence its characters exercised over irresponsible youth; and as long afterwards as 1773 Sir John Fielding found it necessary to appeal to David Garrick not to revive the play which, he said, 'was never presented upon the stage without creating an additional number of real thieves and highwaymen, as witness the increased robberies on Hounslow and Hampstead Heaths.'

Gaming was a worse evil which swelled the ranks of highwaymen. Under the Stuart monarchs gaming became huge and profitable business. Lucky or skilful gamesters, such as Beau Nash, made a respectable living by it, but others, more rash, dissipated great fortunes, ruining themselves and their families. For such men 'the road' was more attractive than a debtors' prison, and offered some chance of recouping part of their losses. From this class of highwayman came the gentlemen, or knights, of the road who gave the profession its early glamour.

In the 18th century the highwayman was a cult figure. In an age when thousands were poor and totally without privilege he robbed the rich, although not with any intention of redistributing their wealth among the needy. At a time when the majority of young men were apprenticed for years to a dull trade and often to a hard master, the highwayman represented a life of free enterprise and adventure, wealth and the admiration of women. And among the idle sons of the rich there were those who indulged in highway robbery for kicks, or undertook a hold-up for a wager. Numerous pamphlets and ballads describing the daring exploits, real or imaginery, of famous highwaymen were among the best-sellers of the day, and did much to promote the legend.

Highwaymen came into prominence in the second half of the 17th century after the upheavals of the Civil Wars. Many of them were men made desperate by circumstances, discharged soldiers, or Cavalier gentlemen impoverished and dispossessed by the new regime. Taking to the road offered a way of making a living and, perhaps, of wreaking some revenge upon their enemies. Conditions were favourable to them. The countryside was still thickly wooded and the roads, ill-made, narrow and winding between trees and hedges, were ideal for surprise attacks. Above all, the only force for law and order was an ancient hue and cry system which made the local inhabitants responsible for pursuing and bringing robbers to justice. A clever, well-mounted highwayman who could shoot straight and ride like the devil had little to fear from rustics busy with their own concerns and unwilling to get involved in violent affairs.

One of the most famous of the Royalist highwaymen sometimes met with on the Bath Road was the self-styled 'Captain' James Hind. Born at Chipping Norton, Oxfordshire, about 1618, and of a respectable family he was apprenticed at the age of 15 to a butcher, but after serving for less than two years he ran away to London in search of a more adventurous way of life. There he fell into bad company and was imprisoned for a while in Poultry Compter where he met a highwayman named Thomas Allen. After their release the two joined forces and carried out many successful robberies together, Hind soon winning a reputation for chivalry by returning one pound out of fifteen he stole from a traveller on Shooter's Hill. During the Civil Wars many stories circulated of

131

"Captain Hind robbing Colonel Harrison in Maidenhead Thicket"

their daring attacks on Cromwell's men but, eventually, Allen was caught and hanged after the two of them had attacked Cromwell himself while travelling in his coach between Huntingdon and London. Hind escaped by hard riding.

Later he joined the Royalist Army and was present at Colchester when it was taken by General Fairfax in August 1648. Hind made good his escape by disguising himself in women's clothes. After the execution of Charles I he made a point of attacking regicides (those who had signed the King's death warrant) and successfully waylaid and robbed Hugh Peters in Enfield Chase, Colonel Harrison in Maidenhead Thicket and Sergeant Bradshaw on Hounslow Heath when on his way to his country seat at Hanworth Park. After robbing them Hind is said to have harangued them on their crimes against the king. In September 1651 he marched with the Royalist forces to the battle of Worcester, and after their defeat escaped to London where he lived for several weeks under an assumed name. In November he was betrayed, arrested and brought before the Speaker of the House of Commons for questioning with regard to his 'late engagement with Charles Stuart, and whether he was the man that accompanied the Scots king for the furtherance of his escape'. Asked whether he had read *Hind's Ramble* and *Hind's Exploits*, two of the many popular pamphlets about him, he replied that although they were fictitious, he had played 'some merry pranks and revels'. He was taken in irons to Newgate and later to Reading, where on 1 March 1652 he was tried for the murder of a man he had shot at Knowl Hill, near Maidenhead, some time before, and whom he had mistaken for a pursuer. The Act of Oblivion (a general pardon for offences committed before a certain date) came into force the next day, but Hind was not allowed to go free. He was removed to Worcester, charged with high treason (not covered by the act) and found guilty. On 24 September 1652 he was hanged, drawn and quartered, the parts of his body exhibited in different parts of the town, and his head displayed on a spike over the gate of the Severn Bridge.

Claude Duval, the ladies' favourite highwayman, belongs to the happier period after the Restoration. Born in Normandy in 1643, he became a servant to an Englishman living in Rouen, and in 1660 came to

England with a party of returning exiles and worked as a footman to the Duke of Richmond. It was not long before he began to mix with bad company, gave up any idea of earning an honest living, and took to the road. Soon he became known for his daring exploits, and especially for his gallantry towards the women whose coaches he waylaid. In fashionable circles numerous stories began to circulate about him, and his female victims were objects of envy to their less fortunate acquaintances. The authorities, however, were not susceptible to his charms, and a list of wanted highwaymen published in the *London Gazette* put his name at the top.

Violence seems to have played little part in his roadside manner, and the classic story which is told about him dancing a coranto with a lady whose husband he robbed is believed to be true, and to have taken place on Hounslow Heath. Having learned that a certain knight and his lady were travelling over the Heath by night and carrying with them the sum of £400, Duval and some of his confederates rode after them and surrounded the coach. The lady, to show that she was not afraid, took a flageolet out of her pocket and began to play a tune. Duval, much amused, produced his own flageolet and also began to play, at the same time moving his horse nearer to the coach. Then, addressing the bewildered knight, he said, 'Sir, your lady plays excellently and I doubt not but that she dances as well. Will you please to walk out and let me have the honour to dance one coranto with her upon the heath?' 'Sir', the knight replied, 'I dare not deny anything to one of your quality and good mind. You seem a gentleman and your request is very reasonable.' With which the knight stepped down from his coach and Duval leaped off his horse and held out his hand to the lady. There, on the moonlit heath, they danced the famous coranto, Duval performing with such exquisite grace and skill that 'the best dancing masters in London could not show such footing as he did in his great French riding boots'. The dance at an end, he escorted the lady back to the coach, but as the knight was stepping in after her he said, 'Sir, you have forgot to pay the music.' 'No. I have not', replied the knight, and thrusting his hand under the seat of the coach he brought out a bag containing a hundred pounds. Duval accepted it courteously saying, 'Sir, you are liberal, and shall have no cause to repent your being so. This liberality of yours shall excuse you the other three hundred pounds.' And giving him the password in case he met with any more of the fraternity on the road that night, he took his leave.

As in the case of other highwaymen who were heroes in their lifetime numerous pamphlets were published about Duval's adventures, recounting the clever tricks he played to separate his victims from their gold, and how he escaped from many tight corners. In later years he seems to have grown more violent and after having robbed the King's Master of Buckhounds of 50 guineas he fled to France with a price upon his head. Later he returned to England where he boldly continued his desperate career as highwayman, card-sharper, gambler and ladies' man, but at last he was captured in totally unromantic circumstances during a drunken brawl at the Hole-in-the-Wall Tavern near the Strand. On 14 January 1670 he was charged with robbery on the King's Highway, stealing the horse and goods of Viscount Grandison, murdering a man named Tirrell, and many more offences. Three days later he was found guilty on at least six charges and sentenced to death. Although fine ladies wept and pleaded for his life, the king would allow no pardon, and Duval was hanged at Tyburn on 21 January, the business being got over so quickly that he had no opportunity to read the speech in praise of his women friends which was later found in his pocket.

Half an hour after his death his body was cut down and taken to a tavern in St Giles, where it lay in candle-lit state and was visited by crowds of people until a judge ordered them to disperse. The body was then taken for burial to St Paul's Church, Covent Garden, where a white marble stone was laid over his grave beneath the centre aisle, bearing an epitaph beginning:

Here lies Duval: Reader, if Male thou art,
Look to thy purse; if Female, to thy heart.

In contrast to such romantic episodes were the grim facts of real incidents, especially as seen from the victim's point of view. Contemporary newspapers contained many advertisements offering rewards for stolen property or for the apprehension of thieves. This one, which appeared in the *London Gazette* of 1 December 1681, is typical and relates to a robbery on the Bath Road.

Robb'd the 10th of Nov. last, from Mr. Joseph Bullock of Bristol, on the Road between Hungerford and Newbury in Barkshire, one Silver Watch and Case, there being on the backside of the Case an Almanack, a Hanger with a Plate Hilt, a Buff Belt, with Silver Buckles; by Three Men, the one a middle-siz'd Man, full Fac'd, a short White Wigg much Curl'd in an old Cloth-Colour riding Coat, on a Flea-bitten Horse, about 14 hands high, his Brows Brown; the other a middle-sized Black Favour'd, on a Grey Horse, about 14 hands high, with Black Hair or Wigg, and thin Favour; the other a full set Man, thin Favour'd with curled dark Brown Hair. Whoever can discover the Persons aforesaid to Mr Bullock of Bristol or at the Three Cups in Breadstreet, London; (the said Robbers having killed one John Thomas, the said Mr Bullock's Servant) shall have their Charges, and ten pounds reward.

Two notorious highwaymen who often worked on the Bath Road were John Hawkins and George Simpson, members of a gang which specialised in mail robberies. In their time the mails were still carried by postboys riding alone with the mail bags strapped to their backs or slung on either side of their saddles. Postboys were easy prey, even if they were grown men instead of young lads, and armed robbers could soon overpower them to snatch the mails for the banknotes which might be concealed within them.

Hawkins was born around 1690, the son of a farmer at Staines. He began his career as a barman at the Red Lion Inn at Hounslow, where he got into the company of thieves and gamesters. After a while he left the Lion to take up a job in a gentleman's house, from which he was dismissed on the suspicion that he had played a part in a robbery of his master's silver. He then took to holding up coaches on the Heath, and at first was very successful on his own. In between robberies he went into hiding in London, where he gambled away all his takings. Later he sought safety in numbers and joined up with a gang of five which soon made a name for itself by robbing stage coaches and postboys on nearly every main road out of London. They were reputed to have held up five coaches bound for Bristol, Gloucester, Oxford, Cirencester and Worcester in one day. From time to time one or more members of the gang was caught and either hanged or given his liberty for providing evidence against the others. Loyalty was not a common virtue among highwaymen.

There was no lack of recruits to the gang, and new members included Hawkins' brother, William, and Ralph Wilson, a former barrister's clerk ruined by gambling. In April 1722 they laid plans for robbing the Bristol mail on Hounslow Heath. The postboys were to be robbed twice, on the 16th and the 18th, so that the gang would stand a good chance of getting both halves of the bank notes being sent that week. The first robbery went off smoothly, but the second was to be their last. An account of how it was carried out survives in the statement made after their arrest by Ralph Wilson. It tells how they lay in wait for the postboy in Langley Broom, a lonely common between Colnbrook and Slough, how they had to alter their plans when the postboy was seen to be riding with another traveller, and how, after the robbery, they made their way by a circuitous route into the heart of London, where they shared out the booty.

About 11 o'clock at night they came to the George at Colnbrook, which was the post-house, and there they ate their supper on horseback. 'We enquired of the ostler what time the Bristol mail would come by, and he told us between one and two in the morning. We went thence, and came to Langley Broom about midnight, where we agreed to dispatch Simpson alone to meet the mail. He went and we loitered about, waiting for his return, and about one o'clock, we saw the post-boy and a traveller with him, and Simpson following them. Then we met Simpson, and held a fresh consultation, in which it was agreed, that Hawkins should watch at a distance, because, he being pretty bulky, would be more remarkable. Then Hawkins and I changed horses, and I and Simpson followed the boy and the traveller through Colnbrook; and on this side of Longford, we rode up to them, and taking hold of their horses bridles, we led them down Harmondsworth-lane, where we made them dismount. I left Simpson to blindfold them, and took the boy's gelding, and mail to the end of the lane, where I found Hawkins waiting, and where in a little time Simpson came to us. We all rifled the bags, and carried several of them to Hounslow-heath, where we selected those of Bath and Bristol, and left the rest. Thence we rode through Kingston and Wandsworth, and going down a bye-road, we searched the bags, and took out what we thought fit, most of which we put into two riding bags, and the rest into our pockets, and what we thought would be of no service to us we put into the Bristol and Bath bags again, and threw them over a hedge. Then taking our way through Camberwell, we came along Greenwich road to the Hand inn, in Barnaby-street, between five and six on Monday morning. There we put up our horses, and drank a pint of burnt wine, and after some time, took coach and drove to the Minories; where, to avoid suspicion, we parted, and went by different ways to Frank Green's, at the Cock and George, in the Minories. We went into a room by ourselves, and to take off all mistrust, we called for a candle, wax, paper, pen and ink, and then locking the door, we examined our prize. We reserved only the bank-notes, and burnt all the other notes and the letters with the candle, which we set in the chimney; we found three £20 bank-notes, one of £25, half of a £50 and two halves of £25 each, which we equally divided. I was apprehended on the Monday following, and made this same confession before Mr Carteret, the post-master general, and by my directions the prisoners were taken at Mrs Bowen's, a midwife, in Green-Arbour-Court, in the

Little Old Bailey.'

Carteret, the Postmaster-General, had been infuriated by this latest robbery of the mails, and determined to catch the men responsible. Ralph Wilson, sitting in the Moorgate Coffee House in the City a few days after the robbery, heard gossip of a great hue and cry. This so alarmed him that he arranged to take a sea passage to Newcastle, but he was traced by one of the stolen notes and arrested before he could board the ship. He was taken immediately to the Postmaster-General himself, to whom he at first denied all knowledge of the robbery, but hearing that Hawkins and Simpson were also in custody, he turned evidence against them, as indeed did Hawkins and Simpson against the others. Wilson's evidence was selected and his neck was saved. Hawkins and Simpson were convicted and hanged on 21 May 1722. Their bodies were afterwards taken to be hung in chains at the end of Longford Lane, near the place where they had caught up with the postboy and his companion.

There was a gibbet, too, overlooking the Bath Road between Beckhampton and Calne, and here the bodies of Wiltshire highwaymen were hung, including members of the notorious Cherhill Gang. This gang, which existed for some years, was based at Cherhill and robbed travellers on the roads from Marlborough to Calne and Devizes. Among stories told of them is one concerning Serjeant Merryweather, a barrister who successfully defended one of the gang at the Assizes. On his way home Merryweather was attacked and robbed; and when the man was caught he was found to be the client whose acquittal he had gained that morning. Another member of the gang was known to leap out from behind bushes stark naked, so startling his victims that robbery was made easier; his lack of clothing also made it harder for people to identify him. In view of the icy winds which blow over the Wiltshire Downs, he probably only worked in the nude on summer nights.

When members of the gang were caught and convicted they were hanged at Devizes, and their bodies were brought to Cherhill Hill to be gibbetted. In such a

A visit to an old acquaintance, from a print by Thomas Rowlandson deserted spot it was easy for their friends and fellow highwaymen to come at night to cut down the gibbet, or clamber up it, to remove the bodies. When this had happened several times, the authorities resorted to binding the lower part of the gibbet with iron, tarring it, and driving in hundreds of nails, which acted as an effective deterrent.

Some of the most brutal attacks on travellers were carried out by footpads armed with bludgeons, who were particularly on the look-out for that most vulnerable of wayfarers, the solitary horseman riding home in the dark along a lonely road. This was how a Berkshire man died one November night in 1784, and his death was reported in the *Reading Mercury*.

Last Sunday morning, between one and two o'clock, Mr Wyatt, a considerable dealer in sheep, of Englefield, in this county, was found dead a little beyond the turnpike on the Newbury road, by one of the Bath coaches. The guard was immediately dispatched back to this town to give information and procure assistance to remove the body; but was surprised, on his returning, to find the deceased almost stripped, and his cloaths carried to some distance; from this it was concluded he had been murdered, and that the coach coming by at the instant prevented the villains from plundering him, but that they had secreted themselves till an opportunity offered for that purpose. The deceased was put into the mail coach from Bristol, and brought to the turnpike-house, where he lay till Monday morning, when the Coroner's inquest sat on the body; and from the evidence of the guard, and several other witnesses, it appeared that Mr. Wyatt had left a publick-house in this town, and had proceeded no farther than the end of Southcot-lane on his return home, before, it is supposed, he was attacked by two footpads, as two men were seen lurking near the fatal spot, about half an hour before, who knocked him from his horse, as on examination his skull was found to be fractured, and he had another bruise on the hinder part of his head. His purse was found in the road the next morning empty; from which and several other concurring circumstances, the jury brought in their verdict, Wilful Murder by some person or persons unknown.

As the deceased had received a considerable sum of money in the course of the day, it is supposed his purse contained near £40. His watch and pocket-book, in which were two Bank Notes, were not taken from him.

Robberies with murder, as in the case of Mr Wyatt, were not uncommon, but in the majority of incidents the victims were physically unharmed and the impression gained from numerous reports in contemporary newspapers and memoirs is that travellers resignedly handed over their money, watches, fobs and trinkets in order to get rid of their assailants. In the *Worcester Journal* in 1738 it was recorded that, between four and five in the morning of 21 September, the Flying Bath Coach was stopped by two footpads about a mile on the London side of Newbury. One of them held the horses' heads while the other robbed all five of the passengers, none of whom offered the least resistance.

Highwaymen were sometimes quite polite. In January 1743 a Captain in the army, travelling to Bath in a post-chaise, was stopped near Sandy Lane by two highwaymen, one of whom asked for a guinea, which he hoped soon to be able to repay him. The Captain gave him a guinea, the fellow gave the driver a shilling and told him if he was stopped by anyone else to say 'Virgin Mary', that being the watchword for the day. They had not gone far before they were stopped by four men; but on being given the watchword, the men raised their hats and rode away.

Other highwaymen were nervous, perhaps when they were novices, or young men playing pranks. In 1751 it was reported that, 'On Saturday morning the Reading Stage-Coach, coming to London, was attacked by a single Highwayman on Maidenhead Thicket, who took from the Passengers about four Pounds. By his behaviour he seemed to be young in the Business, seeming to be greatly frightened and terrified.'

People carrying large sums of money or items of great value concealed them in secret places in their carriages, or about their clothing, keeping a few lesser items ready in case they were obliged to 'stand and deliver'. Some tried more amusing methods. The *Public Advertiser* of May 1766 related that, 'A few nights ago, among the passengers that were going in the stage from Bath to London, were two supposed females that had taken outside places. As they were climbing to their seats it was observed that one of them had men's shoes and stockings on, and upon further search, breeches were discovered also. This consequently alarming the company, the person thus disguised was taken into custody and locked up for the night. The next day he was brought before a magistrate, and upon a strict examination into matters, it appeared that he was a respectable tradesman who, having cash and bills to a large amount on him, thus disguised himself to escape the too urgent notice of the Travelling Collectors.'

Only a few gentlemen did not resign themselves to paying up, but travelled with their pistols ready and did not hesitate to shoot. Lord Berkeley, who went by coach regularly from London across Hounslow Heath to his house at Cranford, was twice held up and made to pay. The third time he was ready, and shot the highwayman dead.

After Hounslow Heath, Maidenhead Thicket was the most dangerous place on the Bath Road. It had enjoyed an evil reputation as far back as the 13th century, when Henry III ordered that both sides of the road through the Thicket were to be kept clear of trees and bushes, but this measure had done little to deter the thieves who infested the area and continued to rob as they pleased.

In the absence of a police force the law with regard to highway robberies placed the onus upon the inhabitants of the division of the county called the Hundred in which a robbery took place. On the raising of hue and cry by the person robbed, the inhabitants were bound either to bring the thieves to justice or, if they failed to do so, to reimburse the victim for his losses. The necessary sums were raised by a rate levied on the parishes, in which people were assessed according to their circumstances. The burden of payment fell particularly heavily upon the Berkshire Hundred of Beynhurst, in which Maidenhead Thicket lay, and in 1597 an Act had been passed for its relief. It was pleaded on behalf of the Hundred that, although it contained five villages (Bisham, Hurley, Remenham, Shottesbrook and White Waltham), none of them was situated on the main highway; neither were there any fields alongside it where men might be working and so be on hand if a robbery took place. Also, the length of the highway was such that men could not continually keep watch over it in order to prevent robberies. To make matters worse, notice of nearly all the robberies taking place was given in the town of Maidenhead, in the adjoining Hundred, so that claims were made against Beynhurst in respect of robberies of which it had received no notice. In one year a total of £255 had been claimed, a heavy charge upon a rural area, and one which had impoverished or ruined many people. The Act allowed that Beynhurst should not be held responsible where it had received no notice of a robbery.

The town of Maidenhead continued to suffer on account of the notorious Thicket; so much so that, in 1736, the landlord of the Bear Inn was authorised to pay £20 reward for information leading to the arrest of highwaymen in the Thicket, and over 60 years later so many robberies were still taking place that the Maidenhead Cavalry, formed for home defence during the wars against Napoleon, resolved to mount guard in rotation and to patrol the roads at night in an attempt to prevent further attacks.

But the laws of hue and cry could be used for fraudulent purposes. The story which follows concerns the operation of hue and cry, not in the Hundred of Beynhurst but in that of Sonning, near Reading; and it reveals the truth behind this notice which appeared in the *London Gazette* of 29 March 1748:

Notice is hereby given, pursuant to the Statute made in the eighth year of his present Majesty's Reign, intitul'd,

An Act for the Amendment of the Law relating to Actions on the Statute of Hue and Cry, That Thomas Chandler of Clifford's Inn, London, Gentleman, on Thursday the 24th Day of March instant, between the Hours of Five and Six of the Clock in the Afternoon of the same Day, as he was travelling on the King's Highway leading from Hare-hatch in Berkshire to Twyford, in the Road to Reading, was robb'd in the Parish of Ruscombe, in the Hundred of Sunning, in the County of Berks, of Fifteen Bank Notes of the Value of Nine Hundred and Sixty Pounds, of Five Guineas in Gold, Twenty Shillings and upwards in Silver, and a Silver Watch, by three Men on Foot, all unknown to him, who obliged him to dismount from his Horse, and took him into a Pit in a Field adjoining to the Highway, and there robbed him. Two of the Robbers were short well-set Men, about Thirty years of Age, and the other was a tall thin Man about Fifty Years of Age: All Three of the Robbers had on light-colour'd Great Coats, and dark brown Wigs.

Thomas Chandler was the son of a gentleman-farmer of Wiltshire, who was sent, about the year 1743, to train as Clerk to a London Attorney. At the office of Mr Hill of Clifford's Inn Thomas worked with so much diligence and sobriety that he won the trust and respect, not only of his master, but of all his clients. In the course of his duties he studied his country's laws to good effect, particularly those relating to highway robbery, and by the time he reached the final year of his clerkship he had worked out a clever plan for making a very considerable amount of money. His plan was to get hold of as large a sum as he possibly could, pretend to be robbed of it, and by that means to double the sum at the expense of the Hundred in which he chose to be robbed.

The initial sum he obtained by deceit; getting £400 from his father by pretending that he was about to be married, and a further £500 from Mr Hill in connection with some legal business on behalf of a client in Wiltshire. He then made arrangements to travel down to Wiltshire to meet the client on Lady Day, 25 March 1748. On the morning of 24 March Thomas collected together all the money he had obtained from various sources, amounting to over £900, and having carried out several confusing exchanges of large and small bank notes, set out about noon along the Bath Road, with the money stowed away in two small canvas bags concealed beneath his garters. Although he had, ostensibly, to cover 90 miles before the morning, he travelled slowly and had got no further than Hare Hatch by 5.30 in the evening. A little way beyond that was the place he had chosen for his 'robbery', and having got rid of his horse, he hid himself in a pit near the road for almost three hours, during which he contrived to bind together his arms and legs. When it was quite dark, he climbed out of the pit and hopped back along the road for half a mile until he met a shepherd, a simple-minded fellow, who believed his story and kindly cut his bonds asunder.

Thomas then asked to be taken to the nearest constable, to whom he gave a written statement concerning the robbery and a description of the three men who, he alleged, were responsible. Three men answering his description, whom he had in fact seen and carefully observed when passing through Maidenhead Thicket, were found but indignantly protested their innocence. 'They would all certainly appear at Abingdon Assizes', they said 'and hang the Dog, for scandalizing three honest Bargemen', (or stronger words to that effect).

Meanwhile, having taken the first essential step towards bringing an action against the Hundred of Sonning, Thomas strolled up the road to the Hare and Hounds, at Hare Hatch, and ordered a good supper and a bowl of punch. After that, he told the Landlord (Mr Butter) his story and desired him to give notice to his neighbours of the robbery and of the victim's intentions. Next morning he rode back to London, pretending to be in a hurry in order to stop payment of the bank notes, but in reality to change one of them at a silversmith's in order to get some ready cash, and to tell a good many involved lies to Mr Hill and everyone else concerned. He also arranged for notices of the robbery to be inserted in the *London Advertiser* and other daily papers on the following morning. On 29 March the official notice printed at the begining of this story appeared in the *London Gazette*.

In order to allow the inhabitants of Sonning Hundred as little time as possible to prepare evidence, he delayed returning to Berkshire to lay information before a Justice until the middle of May, but on the 12th of that month he went, with the still trusting Mr Hill, to present a very detailed account of what he claimed had happened to Mr Hayes, Justice of the Peace of Berkshire, who lived at Holyport.

The time was now approaching for his cause to be tried at Abingdon Assizes, and the principal inhabitants of Sonning Hundred held a meeting at the Rose Inn at Wokingham, where they requested Mr Edward Wise, Attorney of that town, to undertake their defence. The repayment of so large a sum as Chandler claimed to have lost would fall as a heavy charge upon the poorer inhabitants. Wise was a keen and clever lawyer who, by carrying out persistant enquiries at Hare Hatch and in London, soon came to the conclusion that Chandler was an imposter. But, at the trial, Chandler, supported by the innocent Mr Hill, argued his case so convincingly that the jury brought a verdict in his favour. He was awarded £975 damages.

Although greatly pleased with the success of his plan, Chandler took the precaution of moving away from London (a move he had planned some time previously) to an address near Colchester, which he kept secret from all his former acquaintances, and arranged for letters to be forwarded to him by a devious route. At Colchester he changed his occupation to that of innkeeper.

But Edward Wise, the lawyer, had by no means given up the case. For many months he patiently pursued his enquiries, but just as he had almost tracked down his quarry, Chandler moved to Coventry, where he kept another inn. Still Mr Wise, and by now various other interested parties, pursued him, and in the summer of 1750 the law at last caught up with Thomas Chandler. He was brought back to Reading Gaol to await his trial on a charge of wilful and corrupt perjury. This time the weight of evidence against him was overwhelming, and he could make no defence. The jury brought in a verdict of guilty and the judge pronounced the sentence, that he was 'to be set in the Pillory the next Market-Day at Reading, from twelve to one o'clock, and afterwards to be transported for seven years'. Chandler presented a petition to the judge, praying that he might not be set in the pillory, and after some consideration, the first part of his sentence was changed to three months imprisonment. The judge was apprehensive that, if Chandler were put in the pillory, he would be murdered by the angry mob.

Beside the Bath Road between Hare Hatch and Ruscombe there used to be some chalk pits from which materials were extracted for repairing the road. One of them may well have been the pit where Thomas Chandler lay, on the day when he pretended to be robbed.

By the end of the 18th century highwaymen were becoming less common. Indeed, Edmund Burke, who died in 1797, expressed his opinion that the age of highwaymen was over, and the age of cheats had begun. But it was not until the 1830s that highway robbery became a rare occurence. Four things had combined to suppress highwaymen. The refusal by Justices to licence the inns that sheltered them; the enclosure of heathlands where they lay in wait for travellers; the formation of mounted police patrols; and the increasing use of bank cheques which made robbery less profitable.

After the abolition of public hanging the roadside gibbets stood gaunt and empty for many years. Those at Hounslow were cut down about the year 1804, and their stumps were removed when Hounslow tramway was being laid in 1900.

10

The Great Bath Road

Our Roads, in general, are so fine; and our speed has reached the Summit. John Byng, *The Torrington Diaries, June 1791.*

By the end of the 18th century the Bath Road was the finest road in England. After years of continuous maintenance by turnpike trusts it was wider, smoother and firmer, enabling traffic to move very much faster. Hills had been made less steep and rocky, or bypassed; trees and other obstructions had been removed. From Hyde Park Corner to Bath and Bristol, milestones measured the way. Standing taller than most of the stumps which survive today, and clearly lettered, they served as important landmarks for travellers. Together with signposts at road junctions, and the well-defined route, they made the way clear. It would have been difficult to take a wrong turning, as Pepys had done in the previous century; and, indeed, such straying was discouraged by the trusts, whose numerous side gates and bars, put up to prevent people from evading the main toll gates, helped also to keep them in the right road.

Other forces had been at work, contributing to the overall excellence of the road. Town councils, often involved with the trusts, had widened and strengthened bridges, as at Chippenham, or replaced them by new ones, as at Maidenhead. Enclosures of commons and the ploughing up of heaths and thickets had not only reduced the number of places where highwaymen could lurk, but also the opportunities for wayfarers to create alternative tracks. This last was much regretted by horsemen such as Byng, who complained that the new roads were hard, stony and dusty, 'whereas, formerly the horse tracks were good riding, and the side paths numerous; besides all the excellent scampering over the downs, heaths and commons, now so generally enclosed. Depend upon it that riding is ruined by the enclosures and fine rounding of the roads.'

Considered as a means of conveying people from place to place the Bath Road was efficient and well-organised. Fast, reliable stage and mail coaches ran every day. There were first class facilities for travelling post or in private carriages; and travellers enjoyed a very wide choice of inns. Towns and villages provided all the services needed to care for horses and keep vehicles in repair; while the larger towns also offered a variety of amusements for leisure hours.

Scenically it was a pleasant, often beautiful, road, traversing some of the most fertile and prosperous counties of England. Areas under cultivation were interspersed with well-timbered parks surrounding country seats; fine houses could be glimpsed through trees or ornamental gateways; pretty villages lay among lush meadows, with distant prospects of wooded hills. In Wiltshire this gentler scenery gave way to the open, sheep-grazed Downs, with their lonely grandeur; and beyond these the traveller could admire the thickly wooded slopes of the Avon valley as he descended the last long hill into Bath.

In 1792 Archibald Robertson, a minor landscape painter and engraver, published in two volumes the first book about the Bath Road. Its full title, in the grand manner of the time, was *A Topographical Survey of the Great Road from London to Bath and Bristol; with Historical and Descriptive Accounts of the Country, Towns, Villages, and Gentlemen's Seats on and adjacent to it; Illustrated by Perspective Views of the Most Select and Picturesque Scenery.* This book was the first to single out one of Britain's highways as the subject for a whole work, and its publication was a sure sign of the unique importance of the road, and its interest to a large and wealthy section of the public.

Robertson's book was not intended as a practical guide for travellers. Such details as distances between places

Syon Lodge gates, from Robertson's *Great Road to Bath*, 1792

and names of inns and posting houses he left to the compilers of general guidebooks, such as Cary's *New Itinerary*, which were widely available. His purpose was to describe the charms of the scenery and provide 'the curious and inquisitive traveller' with information about the places through which he passed, and the fine houses and objects of antiquity along the way. His maps, showing the road and the country for some distance on either side, are especially interesting today because they show the route of the Bath Road before many alterations, such as those at Cherhill and Derry Hills, had been carried out, and long before many modern bypasses were made. His illustrations show a succession of handsome houses, sylvan landscapes and picturesque town buildings.

At the time he was writing, rural scenes could be enjoyed almost from the start of the journey. In those days, cows grazed and girls picked flowers in Green Park, while all the way from London to Hounslow there were gardens, nurseries and orchards on both sides of the road. Although he thought that Brentford (an unlovely place according to every writer on the Bath Road) had little to boast of besides its situation, being composed of one long street, with houses mostly small and ill-built, he pointed out that the country around it was diversified by cultivation, ornamental villas and wooded scenery. But, even then, London was stretching out long, thin tentacles into the countryside, for he noted an almost continuous chain of buildings, of various dimensions and appearances, extending for more than eight miles from the metropolis.

Descriptions of country houses feature largely in the book, and rightly so, for these and their estates then occupied a considerable proportion of the land. The 18th century had been a period when accumulated wealth had enabled the nobility and gentry to enlarge and embellish their properties, while newly rich merchants and returning Indian Nabobs had been buying up land and building themselves new houses. Sites on or near the Bath Road, with its easy access to London, were sought after. In that century, too, it became possible to build houses on hillsides, allowing proud owners to enjoy views over the surrounding countryside, some of it theirs. As problems with water supplies were solved, there was a general move to higher ground. 'Commanding a prospect' became a fashionable requirement for a house; and there were, of course, the advantages of drier and healthier living conditions. These considerations led to the abandonment of many an ancient house set beside a river or enclosed in a moat, as the family moved uphill into a new mansion. Travellers along the Bath Road could see, or at least could read about in Robertson's book, houses of every size and style, ranging from the neat, dignified homes of the lesser gentry to the palatial establishments of the nobility, whose owners were busy filling them with fine furniture and pictures, and laying out the parks and pleasure gardens according to the latest fashion.

Two of the grandest houses along the road, Syon and Osterley, were situated only a few miles from London. Both were old houses which had been largely rebuilt in the 18th century, and their interiors renovated by Robert

Adam. Robertson pointed out the impressive entrance to Syon, 'ornamented by a beautiful arch, with an open colonade, and a handsome lodge on each side, forming an elegant and picturesque piece of architecture.' For the benefit of those unfortunate people who could see no more than that he described the principal rooms and the grounds, and added a short history of the house. At Osterley he did justice to the sumptuous furnishings, the pictures and the decorations. The lakes and the elegant menagerie of exotic and curious birds were also praised; and so was the rookery, where 'the numerous tribes ... through their hoarse sounding throats, proclaim the happiness and liberty they enjoy, in common with the more beautiful inhabitants of this protected spot.'

Among the many lesser houses near London was Sion Hill, 'an elegant little villa belonging to the Duke of Marlborough.... The grounds are rather contracted, but pleasant and well-wooded; they were laid out under the direction of the late Mr Brown; and extend to the great road.' Near the nine mile stone, on the right, stood a neat house called Spring Grove, the summer residence of Sir Joseph Banks, the famous botanist who had sailed round the world with Captain Cook, and was now President of the Royal Society. At Hounslow, on the edge of the Heath, was Whitton Park, property of the architect Sir William Chambers, whose gardens emulated those of an Italian villa, ornamented with temples, statues and ruins. A little over 12 miles from London was Cranford Park, a seat of the Earl of Berkeley. This was an old-fashioned house set in a corner of a park, near the church, and its grounds were thickly wooded and watered by the River Crane. Robertson remarked that it commanded no variety of prospects, but conceded that 'from the distribution of the woods, and other accompaniments, it may be deemed a pleasant retirement.' Pheasant abounded there, and considerable pains were taken by the noble proprietor for their preservation.

Near Slough were Langley Park, the seat of Sir Robert Bateson Harvey, a handsome stone house set in the centre of a pleasant park abounding in fine trees; and

The approach to Maidenhead Bridge

Ditton Park, a venerable house surrounded by a moat. Slough itself was a large village composed chiefly of one street; 'the houses are tolerably built, and it contains some good inns.' On the left of the turning leading to Windsor and Eton stood the house of Dr Herschel, the celebrated astronomer. In his garden, where he had cut down all the trees to make room for it, stood his giant telescope, supported in a wooden frame. It could be seen clearly from the high road, and the King, who had granted £2,000 towards it, had visited it, as had many other notable people.

Along the whole length of the Bath Road through Buckinghamshire Robertson's attention was much taken up with Windsor Castle, glimpses of which could be obtained here and there, and which contributed, he said, 'to cheer the mind of the traveller after the dreary waste of Hounslow Heath.' Approaching Slough the views became more open, but he complained that those towards the Castle were 'too much broken and interrupted by a tiresome continuation of scattered trees.' At last the majestic edifice could be seen in all its glory, 'standing conspicuously on a high hill, the base of which is washed by the most beautiful river in this or any other country ... It's solemn and majestic appearance impresses the mind of the beholder with awe and veneration; and its situation seems to have been pointed out by nature for the seat of monarchs.'

Beyond Salt Hill the scenery became more picturesque, and the wooded hills around Taplow came into view. Several handsome houses ornamented the hillsides, including Taplow House, 'embosomed in wood', the stately mansion of Cliveden, and Hedsor Lodge, the seat of Lord Boston, 'an elegant modern building, loftily situated.' Continuing along the Thames Valley the road between Maidenhead and Reading was 'pleasingly diversified by farms, cottages and some elegant houses.' Bear Place, near Hare Hatch, was the modern residence of Mr Ximenes. Built on rising ground, with open and extensive views towards the south and east, it had replaced a brick and timber house surrounded by a moat. Opposite Bear Place, stood a neat house on a sloping lawn, the residence of Mr James Leigh Perrot, the uncle, (although Robertson naturally did not know this) of Jane Austen, then aged about 17. Mr and Mrs Leigh Perrot were regular visitors to Bath, and must have found their house very conveniently situated for the journey.

The road next ran through Twyford, but finding little to interest him there, Robertson digressed to Wargrave, where the Earl of Barrymore had a house and a small private theatre, recently built and lavishly decorated. There the Earl and a company of mixed amateur and professional players performed for the entertainment of his friends and neighbours.

Around the large and populuous town of Reading the country was 'finely diversified by gentlemen's seats, woody hills, and cultivated land; and the Thames gliding through beautiful meadows, encompasses the northern part of the town.' Across the Thames Caversham Park House could be seen, standing nobly on a hillside. A classical mansion which had been much altered, its present owner was Mr Marsac, who had made his fortune in India. The grounds had, until lately, been adorned by many majestic and venerable trees, but these had been cut down, to the regret of everyone except the owner. On the left, before descending the hill into Reading, was Erleigh Court, an ancient house with a new Georgian front; and nearby was Whiteknights, recently transformed into one of the first examples of the *ferme ornée*. On the western side of the town were Coley Park and Calcot Park, two further examples of houses which had been built in the 18th century to enable their owners to move out of ancestral homes beside a river.

The Kennet Valley now lay to the south as the road ran through Theale, a neat village skirted by fertile meadows, beyond which a chain of wooded hills closed the horizon. To the north-west was Englefield House, the stately mansion of Richard Benyon, Esq. Thatcham, 'a small neat town, chiefly composed of one street, having some good houses and a small church', was followed by Newbury, 'a large and populous town ... situated in a fertile plain, watered by the Kennet ... The streets are spacious and well paved; it contains many good houses, a large church; and the market-house, over which is the guildhall, is a noble building.'

Near Speen, William Brummell, Esq., retired from government service, and father of the future Beau Brummell, then at Eton, had made the most of the charming site of Donnington Grove. His house was a handsome modern one in the Gothic style, situated on a sloping lawn. The Lambourn stream, running in front of the house, had been enlarged into a fine sheet of water, over a mile long, and studded with small islands, the haunt of numerous wildfowl. Behind the house could be seen a ridge of wooded hills and the ruined towers of Donnington Castle. About a mile further, on the left, were the lodge gates of Benham Park, a seat of Lord Craven. The drive descended through a wood to the house, 'a regular mansion of the Ionic order, having an elegant portico on the south front. It is built on a sloping bank, embosomed in a deep and solemn grove,

Lord Craven's house at Benham

composed of trees of various kinds. On the south lies a piece of water, supplied by the Kennet; over which is a handsome wooden bridge in the Chinese taste.' Benham had been built and the grounds laid out by Lord Craven according to the wishes of his wife, the beautiful Elizabeth, who subsequently left him in order to pursue a literary and scandalous career in London and on the Continent. Immediately after Lord Craven's death she married the Margrave of Anspach and, in 1792, returned to live with him at Benham.

In Wiltshire were two of the largest estates bordering the Bath Road. Tottenham Park together with the Forest of Savernake belonged to Lord Ailesbury, and measured at least 12 miles in circumference. The house, a 'regular, handsome structure', replaced one burned down by the Parliamentary forces in the Civil Wars. In the forest, solitary shepherds could be seen wandering with their flocks, and numerous herds of deer 'stamping this spot with a characteristic dignity not to be met with in a less magnificent territory.' Just outside Calne was Bowood where Lord Shelburne and his son, the Marquess of Lansdowne, had greatly enlarged the house and employed Capability Brown to lay out the grounds in a style 'to represent beautiful nature with nothing done to it.'

At Corsham was the fine stone mansion of Paul Methuen, Esq., already housing the famous picture collection of his cousin, Sir Paul Methuen, Ambassador to Spain and Portugal. On the opposite side of the road was Hartham Park the seat of Lady James. The house had been completely altered since, some 30 years before, the park had been cut up by the new road from Corsham into Bath. Continuing on this road through Box, and descending the hill, Robertson very democratically pointed out on the right, about a mile away, 'a handsome house with wings, the residence of Mr Wiltshire; who here enjoys with his amiable family, the fruits of a long series of honest industry and perseverance; having raised himself to his present state of ease, affluence, and respectability, from one of the lowest situations in life, – from the driver, to being the proprietor of the Bath and Bristol waggons.'

Robertson dedicated his book to the Prince of Wales,

The Bath Road through Chippenham

who had visited Bath in 1790, and was to go there again in 1797 and 99. But Bath was no longer a favourite place with royalty. George III preferred Cheltenham or Weymouth, and Bath, in spite of its beauty and all its advantages, was going out of fashion. In 1783 the Prince, aged 21, had first sampled the freer airs of Brighton, and within a few years he was to make that seaside village as brilliant and lively a place as Bath had formerly been.

New medical opinion as well as changing tastes contributed to the decline of Bath. Sea bathing was then being promoted as enthusiastically as taking the waters at inland spas had been in the previous century. Brighton, Weymouth, Lyme Regis, Margate, Scarborough and other 'fishing holes', as Byng disparagingly called them, were growing into smart resorts. There increasing numbers of England's growing population chose to disport themselves, enjoying the new excitements of a dip in the sea and the exploration of coastal scenery.

The character of Bath had changed; and it had, in a sense, grown old. Success had made it too popular, driving away the better-class visitors, and making it more a place of residence for pretentious snobs, elderly invalids and retired professional people. It was thus that Dickens satirised it in *Pickwick Papers*. His Master of Ceremonies, Angelo Cyrus Bantam, Esq., is a ridiculous figure, vulgarly over-dressed and over-scented; drawling his 'Welcome to Ba-ath, sir', to Mr Pickwick, and pressing him to attend a ball in the Assembly Rooms. 'The ball nights in Ba-ath are moments snatched from Paradise; rendered bewitching by music, beauty, elegance, fashion, etiquette, and – and – above all, by the absence of tradespeople, who are quite inconsistent with Paradise.' The company at the ball that evening is composed of 'a vast number of queer old ladies and decrepid old gentlemen', knots of silly young men, match-making mammas and middle-aged spinsters. When Mr Pickwick tactlessly refers to a turbaned dowager as 'the fat old lady', he is instantly rebuked by the Master of Ceremonies. 'Hush, my dear sir – nobody's fat or old in Ba-ath.'

As Bath's glory faded, the coaching age, too, neared its

end. The highest speeds possible with the use of horses had been achieved; and that only at enormous cost to countless generations of these noble animals. In the 1820s and 30s experiments were carried out with horseless carriages, powered by steam. On 28 July 1829 Sir Goldsworthy Gurney, one of the leading inventors, undertook a trial run along the Bath Road with his patent steam tractor. It drew an ordinary barouche, and was alleged to move at the rate of 16 miles an hour. Unfortunately for Gurney, he and his crew reached Melksham on the day of the annual fair, and a crowd of boisterous rustics, shouting 'Down with machinery', stoned the engine, the barouche and its occupants. The engine was temporarily put out of action and some of the party were badly injured, but this did not prevent them from making the return journey to London, covering the 84 miles from Melksham to Cranford Bridge in ten hours. The time included ten stops to take on water and coke.

A few years later all such experiments were forgotten in the widespread enthusiasm for another kind of steam transport running along a different kind of road.

11

The Coming of the Railways

Alas! We shall never hear the horn sing at midnight, or see the pike-gates fly open any more.
W.M. Thackeray *Vanity Fair, ch. 7.* 1848

Towards the end of April 1833, one of the guests staying at the old Bear Inn at Reading was Mr Isambard Kingdom Brunel, newly appointed Engineer of the Great Western Railway. He was engaged in making a survey and plans of the route of the proposed line between Bristol and London, on which Reading was to be an important station. From there, as from Maidenhead, Slough, Twyford, Chippenham and Bath, the travelling public would be able to enjoy a mode of transport twice as fast, and much cheaper, than any coach running along the Bath Road.

If Mr Tagg, landlord of the Bear, could forsee what effect his guest's activities would have upon the roads, and upon old-established inns such as his, he must have been a very worried man. At that time, however, he may well have hoped that all the rumours circulating would come to nothing. After all, the difficulties might prove insurmountable, the scheme would be enormously expensive, and most of the local gentry and farmers who patronised his inn were strongly opposed to it. Five months later, matters were looking more serious. Brunel's plans had been approved, the Great Western Railway Company had been formed, and shares were being advertised in the newspapers. By tradition the Bear was the meeting place of the local Tories, and so it was fitting that, in December that year, a crowded anti-railway meeting was held there, attended by landowners whose estates and farms would be cut up by the proposed line. The meeting resolved unamimously that the railway would be 'injurious to their interests, repugnant to their feelings, and that no case of public utility had been made out to justify such an uncalled-for encroachment upon the rights of private property.'

This meeting was only one of many held across the country by people opposed to the line. Coach proprietors and goods carriers as well as innkeepers stood to lose by the railway. The turnpike trusts, the Kennet and Avon Canal Company, and the Thames Commissioners would all feel the loss of tolls, and so would the town council of Maidenhead, which collected tolls on its bridge over the Thames. Other powerful voices joined in the opposition; the Provost of Eton, for instance, expressed his opinion that the railway might have a demoralising effect on the boys. 'If the boys could be carried to a distance of five miles in fifteen minutes', he said at a meeting at Salt Hill, 'they could easily put themselves out of the reach of the authorities, and so the school must be injured.' But public opinion in the towns, and particularly among merchants and businessmen, was in favour of the line; and after two years of lively controversy, the Great Western Railway Act was passed in Parliament in August 1835.

Maidenhead was chosen as the terminus of the first section of line to be opened. In 1834 the railway company had caused a census to be taken of the traffic passing through this town, and the results had suggested that this was the busiest place on the Bath Road. Over a two-week period the figures were as follows:–

118 pairs of post horses
2230 horses drawing vans and wagons
776 coaches drawn by 4 horses
47 coaches drawn by 2 horses
85 private carriages with horses
456 gigs

287 horses drawing market carts
21 horses drawing carts laden with timber
42 miscellaneous horses
34 horses drawing coal carts
31 horses drawing hay carts
22 horses drawing straw carts
102 beasts
2803 sheep
38 pigs

In order to protect the tolls on the bridge, the first station, a temporary structure, was built a quarter of a mile to the east of the river; and when the line was opened beyond this, the railway company agreed to pay Maidenhead Town Council compensation for the loss of tolls for six years. On Whit-Monday 4 June 1838, the first Maidenhead station was opened to the public, and no less than 1,479 people took the opportunity to try the new form of transport, while thousands of others gathered at vantage points to watch the trains go by.

In July 1839 a station was opened at Twyford, and in March 1840 at Reading, amid scenes of great excitement and enthusiasm. The continuing opposition of Eton College delayed the opening of a station at Slough, but trains were allowed to stop there and passengers bought their tickets at the old Crown Inn. After a while the College gave in, and Slough station was opened in 1840. For several years Slough was the nearest station to Windsor, and used by many important persons when the Court was in residence. For this reason an imposing hotel, named The Royal, was built opposite the station entrance. Meanwhile, construction of the line had proceeded quickly, and by June 1841 the Great Western Railway was completed as far as Bath and Bristol.

The public wasted no time in transferring its custom from the road to the railway, for the lure of speed, and its enormous advantages, were irresistible. Travel became the rage, and people undertook journeys which they would not have dreamed of before, simply because they

The Royal Hotel at Slough, the nearest station for Windsor, about
1845. In the foreground is the loading bay where coaches were put
onto the trains

were now possible. The railway company, in its determination to attract travellers from every level of society, neatly divided them into first, second and third class. For the wealthy ones, luxuriously upholstered carriages with plate-glass windows were provided, and special trucks and horse-boxes were added to the train, so that private carriages could be transported with their owners, for use at the end of the railway journey. Comfort was not something accorded to second class passengers, whose accommodation was described as very like the inside of a stage coach, but the seats were of painted wood and there was no glass in the windows. Third class passengers were carried in open trucks, without the benefit of roof or seats, and being placed at the front of the train near the engine, were exposed to smoke and sparks as well as the elements. They were no more uncomfortable, however, than riding on the top of a stage coach in bad weather, and at least their ordeal was over in less than half the time, and was a lot cheaper.

Coach proprietors were quick to realise that feeding passengers to the railway was their only means of compensating for the loss of custom on routes duplicated by the line; and as soon as the first station was opened at Maidenhead, the more enterprising of them were ready with plans for combined services. William Hone & Co. of Reading, now describing his office in King Street as General Coach and Great Western Railway Office, started a new daily service between Reading and Maidenhead station, timed to catch the morning trains to Paddington, and to await the arrival of returning trains in the afternoon. Their coach was named The Railway. At the same time, Messrs Botham and Nelson, operating coaches from the Pelican at Speenhamland, a good 30 miles away, advertised 'First rate travelling to London, through Woolhampton, Reading and Maidenhead, and thence on the Railway'. Their Optimus Coach left the Pelican every weekday morning for Maidenhead, where it was put on board the train. From Paddington it completed the journey to the proprietors' usual terminus at the Belle Sauvage in Ludgate Hill. The journey was advertised to take 4½ hours. In the afternoon the Optimus left the Belle Sauvage and made its way via the New White Horse Cellar in Piccadilly to Paddington, in time to catch the 4 o'clock train back to Maidenhead. Intending passengers were warned that they must be punctual to time, as the railway trains admitted no delay.

Another service which made use of the special facilities for carrying coaches and horses on the trains was The Beaufort, proudly announced by Messrs J.J. Tagg, Edward Sherman and W. Lane & Co., in June 1838. 'This new and superb conveyance to Bath' set out from the Bull and Mouth in London at 8 every morning to catch the 9 o'clock train to Maidenhead. From there it continued along the Bath Road through Calne and Chippenham, to reach the Lion Hotel in Bath at 6.30 p.m., a total journey time of 10½ hours. The proprietors were 'gratified by the hope that after the establishment of this coach the want of a first rate conveyance to and from Bath will no longer be experienced by its fashionable frequenters.' Mr Tagg, part owner of the Beaufort and landlord of the Bear in Reading, continued to run his own coach called The Star from Reading to Bath every day.

In August 1838 it was announced that the famous Emerald Bath and Bristol stage-coach had been removed from its regular run along the turnpike road from London to Maidenhead, and would be conveyed from Paddington as far as Maidenhead station on the railway, with its passengers and luggage loaded on board as usual. Within a fortnight, two other Bath and Bristol stages were to share the same ignominious fate.

Competing with the railway proved hopeless. The cost of running the coaches was too high, and the numbers of passengers they could carry were too small compared with those borne by the railway. As main lines were completed all over the country, coach proprietors were forced to take their coaches off long-distance routes, and to operate only on minor routes. The last through stage-coach from Bristol to London ran in 1843. After that, it was not long before branch railway lines began to make the minor coach routes redundant as well, putting coach companies out of business altogether. Branch lines which further reduced traffic on the Bath Road were the Newbury and Hungerford branch from Reading, opened in 1847, the Windsor branch from Slough in 1849, and the Marlborough line in 1864.

An even greater loss to the Bath Road was the end of the mail coach service. The contractors who operated the mails had always depended upon the income from passenger fares and parcel carriage, and when this was transferred to the railway they found themselves unable to continue running. The Post Office tried to overcome the problem by putting mail coaches onto trains, but at least one of them came to grief in April 1840, when the Bristol mail coach, on its way from London, caught fire, probably from sparks from the engine. It was reported that 'the guards exerted themselves in every possible way by blowing their horns and calling out to the conductor to stop the train, but they could not succeed in making him hear, and the consequence was that when they arrived at Twyford the whole of the front boot was on fire, and of the contents everything consumed.' After 1 May that year all the mail from Reading to London was carried by rail, and when the line was completed to Bristol in 1841 the coach service ceased altogether on that route.

The loss of the coaching business was a calamity to the smaller places on the Bath Road, such as Hounslow, Longford, Colnbrook, Theale, Thatcham and Beckhampton, which had depended almost entirely upon it. To towns like Maidenhead and Reading the loss was not quite so serious, because the railway instantly replaced the road and, in time, brought even greater benefits to local trade and industry. To the inns, however, the railway brought no advantages. Speedier travel meant that people required hotel accommodation less than before, and this, together with the falling off of the coaching trade, brought ruin to many old-established inns.

The effect on the Bath Road was catastrophic. The daily coaches, with their regular stops, stream of

Steamed out, or the starving stage-coachmen and boys, from an engraving by George Cruickshank

passengers and endless demand for horses, had been the life-blood of the road. Without them it was desolate, its facilities largely disused, its innkeepers closing their doors, and their servants idle or looking for employment elsewhere. It was true that private vehicles and carriers' wagons were still numerous, and continued to be so until well into the age of the motor car, but they were used mostly for short journeys and brought little trade to the inns. Some idea of the devastating effect of the railway on the Bath Road can be gained from a letter written by a lady, describing a journey from Wiltshire to London in January 1844.

Thomas's Hotel, Berkeley Square.

My Dear Kathleen,

You will see that I have arrived in town, after an adventurous journey by road. My state of mind would not permit me to travel by rail, for Mr. Brunel is no hero of mine, since he has destroyed posting, put down coaches and compelled people to sit behind his puffing monsters. Two days have passed since Belinda and I left our home ... You could not imagine that we two women were allowed to take a lengthy journey on deserted roads with the bare possibility of getting horses. I had hoped that we should make London before night, but there was always the possibility of a fog. Just think of the awful risk of damp beds, and no one sleeps at inns since the railway has been cut. 'We sha'n't get to Reading before three, unless we get horses,' said Belinda as we seated ourselves in the barouche, 'and we shall certainly have to sleep on the road.' We admired the country, noted the heavy frost, and talked over our neighbours' affairs until we came to the end of the first stage ... We drew up at the Golden Lion, [at Marlborough] which ten years since was one of the busiest inns on the road. The inn looked deserted – no ostler, no horses ready saddled as in the times when we were children and landlords took a real pride in their stables. We looked at each other in consternation. 'Any horses?' shouted Richard. The landlady, a slatternly person in curl-papers, came out in a slip-shod way. 'No', was plainly written on her face. She seemed surprised to see an old-fashioned travelling carriage and four. 'No, milady, we are new people. We are just come into the house. The people afore us was ruined. Since the railroad came this way nobody wants horses.' 'Will you please to alight, milady', said the elder postilion, a man of about fifty-five, still called a boy; 'we'd take you on another stage if so be you'd bait an hour. The horses would be fresh enough.' There was no alternative, so we descended and followed the landlady into the guest rooms ... The hour passed, and once again we took our seats, this time not so excitedly. We were now on the worst stage, a particularly hilly one, and the surface of the road had been neglected by the turnpike trust. 'Ah,' thought I, 'they will never make another cutting, they will not undertake systematic levelling or throw another bridge across a hollow. Thirty years from now the roads will be as bad as they were in our grandfather's days ... So we jogged on to the end of the next stage. We stopped only a few yards from another inn, the Red Lion [at Hungerford]. Here we found slightly better comfort, for the inn is on a cross route and still boasts a two-horse coach, and we were fortunate enough to secure a change of horses which carried us to Newbury, where we made a halt until further horses could be obtained from a livery stable. On, once more, two stages to Reading, and then another change. The light was failing; what with delays and bad cattle, it was dark when we drew near a small tavern eight miles beyond. The inn in the village seemed busy enough; the landlord said it was a great struggle to keep things going, but he protested on the cleanliness of his rooms and the aired state of his beds. With wondering steps we followed the woman-waiter upstairs into the bedroom and waited in misery while she lit the fire. The woman said it was 'the worst grate in the house, only after a bit it would burn up'. It was cold comfort for two women, who had spent the day under such difficulties... We made preparations for dinner, and on this being announced we made our way to the coffee room... We found an old-fashioned mahogany table in the centre of the coffee room large enough to hold twenty. There was a sideboard covered with all sorts of utensils that bumped, rattled and shook like one of Mr. Brunel's trains every time the woman-waiter stamped about. At last came the mutton, smoking hot and tender, followed by a pudding tasting strongly of onions. This dinner, such as it was, compensated for all the injuries we had gone through ... Next morning we packed into the barouche and in three stages reached London, not experiencing any difficulty with horses...

Ever your loving friend,
Marjorie St. Aubyn.

In the late 1840s huge sales were held of coach horses, coaches, post-chaises and pieces of harness. Many unwanted vehicles never found a buyer, and were left to moulder and rot in deserted coach-houses and inn-yards. The inns died slowly. Only a few closed when the coaching age ended. One of these was the Castle at Marlborough, which closed in 1843 and later became part of Marlborough College. Others lingered on for many years, their landlords making a living as best they could. In 1865 the old Sun Inn at Maidenhead, formerly the most important coaching inn on the Bath Road through that town, was put up for sale by auction. Its tenant at that time was William Hall, described as 'innkeeper and fly proprietor'. He was one of many town innkeepers who retained a humble interest in transport, sending flies to meet trains or hiring them out for short local journeys. Other large old inns, with most of their rooms shut up, survived only as public houses, as did the Bear at Reading (now demolished), the Red Lion at Maidenhead and the King's Head at Thatcham, both still in existence. Some inns were adapted to other uses. The Pelican at Speenhamland became a livery stables and a veterinary establishment before it was demolished in the present century. Others were converted into private houses, including the King's Arms at Speenhamland, the Castle at Speen, the Beckhampton Inn, the Crown at Hungerford, which survives as a farm, and the Castle at Salt Hill. A few, such as the Angel at Woolhampton, survived into the 20th century only to be knocked down to widen the Bath Road; and demolition to make way for modern developments has been the fate of many others. G.C. Harper, describing in the 1890s the dreary aspect of the once bustling main street at Hounslow, wrote: 'The curtailed remains of its once numerous and extensive coaching inns are become, as a rule, low pot-houses, in which labourers in the market gardens that practically surround the town, sit and drink themselves stupid in the evening.'

In 1877 the Windmill Inn at Salt Hill, known for many years as Botham's after the name of the proprietor, was put up for auction, and an elderly gentleman who had known it in the days of the Eton Montem went to have a last look at this famous inn. 'It is strange', he wrote, 'to wander through the great house (they could make up thirty-five beds) and look into rooms still containing the furniture with which the late proprietor commenced life – old prints which, if they could speak, would have strange tales to tell. In a word, any one knowing the *then* could revive it in the *now* were he to revisit the place. He would be puzzled to find any other alteration indoors save the ominous stillness. Breakfasts and dinners were bustling affairs in those old coaching and posting days. But let us revisit the yard, and what a sad change we find. Here the enormous amount of stabling is mostly in ruins. Where seventy pairs of posters stood, one horse, and one alone, is found to do the present fly work of the establishment. Wandering through the old yard, we came upon a coach-house wherein stood five carriages, which had evidently not been moved for many years. So quaint was their build, they would puzzle and delight the antiquary ... In another coach-house was about two waggon-loads of old posting harness, with some postboys' jackets, covered with dust and in every stage of decay. Ascending a staircase, we entered the sleeping-rooms allotted to the postilions; there in rows were the low bedsteads, the canvas moth-eaten, an old lantern lying probably just where it had been thrown after use for the last time years before, and the rooms, save for dust and decay, the same as their occupants left them forever.'

Botham's was sold and was to be converted into a school, but during the night of 21 April 1882, when it was being prepared for its new occupants, some mattresses put in front of a fire to air fell over, and the whole house was burned to the ground. A new Windmill was later built nearby.

The railways brought about the downfall of the turnpike trusts, which had already undergone considerable reorganisation in attempts to make them more efficient. Lengths of road had been transferred from one trust to another, and small trusts had been amalgamated with larger ones. Thus the Bath Road through Reading, from Twyford to Theale, was now administered by the same trust, which had also taken over the road from Theale to Pangbourne, originally turnpiked by a small independent trust, which had erected a gate and toll-house in Tidmarsh. The main turnpike gate in Reading had been moved, about 1830, from Castle Street to a position half a mile west along the Bath Road (near the present Gatehouse Hotel), although it was still known as Castle Street Gate. Similar changes took place around other towns.

A government enquiry in 1839 into the possible effects of railways on the trusts concluded that they had already been materially affected. A statement of debts showed that trusts in England and Wales were in debt to the tune of £9 million, and this figure was fast increasing. Since 1822 turnpike trusts had been obliged by law to present their accounts annually to the local Clerk of the Peace, and these revealed only too clearly how income from tolls fell off after the railways were opened. The following examples are taken from the accounts of trusts maintaining the middle sections of the Bath Road. In 1832 tolls at Twyford Gate, between Maidenhead and Reading, amounted to £1215; at Castle Street Gate £1484, and at Tidmarsh Gate £83. At Thatcham Gate, between Reading and Speenhamland, tolls amounted to £1280; at Hoe Benham Gate, between Speenhamland and Marlborough, £1160. By 1852 these figures had fallen to: Twyford Gate £234; Castle Street and Tidmarsh Gates combined £681; Thatcham Gate £263; Hoe Benham £216.

Always resented, turnpikes in the 1850s became the target of a vociferous campaign for their abolition. In an age of social and economic reform, turnpike gates were seen as obnoxious impositions and intolerable nuisances. Agitation was particularly strong in London, described in a popular catchphrase of the abolitionists as 'the city of a hundred gates'. *The Times* led the press in what was seen as a fight for freedom. 'There is nothing that an Englishman hates more than to be stopped in his progress', ran a leader in October 1856. 'This is mainly the cause of that disgust which the vision of a Turnpike-Gate infallibly creates in the mind of every true-born Briton.' Another fighter, *The Illustrated London News*, in June 1857, said, 'Whether in town or country, the Toll-bar is a barbarous nuisance. Money must, of course, be had for

the construction and repairing of highways; but is it
necessary to collect it on that old system of *stand and
deliver*, in which Claude Duval and Dick Turpin were
such illustrious adepts?'

On 1 July 1864 an act came into force abolishing
turnpike gates and bars on fifty miles of roads around
London. Kensington and Hammersmith gates, through
which the Bath Road traffic had passed, were among
those removed. The roads became the responsibility of
the ratepayers. During the next decade, trusts all over the
country were wound up a few at a time, and their gates
removed. Toll-houses, in places where they were merely
wooden huts, or cottages obstructing the road, were also
taken away. When Corsham Trust (an amalgamation of
the Blue Vein and Bricker's Barn Trusts) was wound up
in 1870, their toll-houses at Blue Vein, Pickwick and
Lacock were each sold for £50; the one in Box,
obstructing the main street, was pulled down.

In many places the removal of the hated gates took
place amid scenes of public rejoicing. At Hounslow, on
the last night of the tolls in July 1872, about 100 people
were seen, just before midnight, converging on the toll-
house near the Bell Inn, where the gates crossed the
Staines and Bath Roads. The toll-keeper, apprehending
danger, absconded with the last day's takings, which were
said to be unusually large, about five minutes before
midnight. The crowd waited patiently till the church
clock gave the first stroke of twelve. Then several of them
made a rush at the gates, lifted them from their hinges,
and bore them off in triumph.

The most elaborate celebrations were staged at
Devizes in 1868, and were described in the *Illustrated
London News* of 14 November.

'On the evening of Saturday, October 31 (the last day of
the Tolls) just before midnight, a band of music went
round to all the gates, playing various airs at each, and
concluding with the National Anthem.

On the evening of the 5th November, the gates, which
had been purchased at the sale of the Turnpike Trust
property, were handed round the town in a waggon

The old toll-gates across the Bath and Exeter roads at Hounslow, about 1864. In the background, the Bell Inn

drawn by four horses and dressed with flags and evergreens, and were then drawn to the top of a high hill two miles from the town, where they were immolated on a bonfire built of an immense pile of faggots, over which a hundred gallons of tar had been poured...

Sky rockets and other fireworks accompanied the bonfire. But the great demonstration was reserved for Friday night, when Professor Gyngell, of Wells, gave a grand pyrotechnic display on Devizes Green, in the presence of several thousands of spectators. In addition to the usual ornamental fireworks, such as may be seen at other displays, there was one designed especially for this occasion ... a brilliant design representing a Turnpike Gate, composed of little jets of diamond light, which after burning some time was destroyed by maroons, or imitative cannon, when the motto 'missed but not wanted' was displayed in diamond and turquoise lights. The Turnpike Gate was 16 or 18 feet long, and was a very beautiful object as long as it lasted, which is, perhaps, more than can be said of the originals.'

12

The Road Revived

As you drive on a main road, traffic drawing you ahead and pushing you behind, you cannot bother a great deal about a road's history. On this Bath Road you drive past history, past its monuments, or you drive through history at 40, 50, 60 miles an hour.
Geoffrey Grigson in *Country Life*, 26 April 1956.

Long before the last toll-gates were removed the Bath Road had become a peaceful rural highway, winding dusty white across the landscape, and passing quietly through villages to which it had formerly brought life, trade and regular links with the outside world. Long distance road transport had ceased altogether. A generation had grown up which could not even remember the dashing mail coaches, the crowded stage coaches, the elegant crested carriages of the nobility, and the great lumbering goods wagons drawn by teams of horses. In place of these were utilitarian gigs, dog-carts, carriers' carts and farm wagons; and sometimes the local gentry driving past in staid barouches drawn by two horses. As it turned out, the carriers were among the hardiest survivors of the railway age, some of them continuing to run right through to the motor age on short routes to villages not served by railways.

The Bath Road began to revive in the 1870s with the growing popularity of the bicycle, a vehicle at first considered so perilous that only a foolhardy young man would attempt to ride it. The much safer tricycle encouraged more cautious people to venture on the roads, but this was slow and cumbersome, and the demand for speed led to the invention of the famous penny-farthing, whose huge wheel, four or five feet in diameter, with pedals on the hub, was capable of giving riders some spectacular falls. The advent of the 'safety bicycle' in 1887, and of pneumatic tyres in the following year, made bicycles suitable for women, and in the 1890s cycling became a craze with both sexes. On fine summer holidays thousands of young enthusiasts left the towns to explore the countryside at leisure, enjoying the exhilerating exercise and the freedom of mile upon mile of quiet roads.

The formation of numerous cycling clubs encouraged cycle racing and tests to find out how quickly distances between major towns and cities could be covered. The Bath Road, flat and gently winding for most of its length, and still possessing a reasonably good surface, was ideal for this purpose, and the journey from London to Bath and back soon became a standard test ride. In 1870 two intrepid pioneers took five days to complete the trip, but such were the advances in design during the next ten years that, in 1880, Wat Britten, riding a penny-farthing, did it in only 23 hours, little more than 2½ times the modern record of 9 hours, 3 minutes and 7 seconds achieved by John Woodburn in 1981.

For 80 years the Bath Road east of Savernake Forest attracted racing cyclists from all over the country to take part in time trials – unpaced riding over an exactly measured distance against the clock. At first, events started near Hounslow and brought a good deal of welcome weekend trade to caterers in that area. The countryside near London was then still so pleasant that several inns around Cranford were advertised as 'an ideal place to stay when you have finished racing.' The dead flat 25 mile course allowed much faster times than were possible on any other road near London. About 1920 increasing motor traffic forced the racing cyclists westwards, and later years saw events starting at Pangbourne Lane, which joins the Bath Road near Theale. The Bath Road 100-mile race, regarded as the cyclists' Blue Riband event and traditionally held on August Bank Holiday Mondays, started from here, and attracted the country's fastest riders. Competitors particularly enjoyed the final 28 mile dash back from Froxfield, which could prove very fast indeed, especially with a following wind. In the 1970s the installation of traffic lights in Thatcham ruined the cycle racing courses, and although some events now start from Speen Hill, the Bath Road has almost lost its classic status.

Early cyclists had had to put up with a good deal of derision and, more seriously, indignant protests from ratepayers, who were again, through the new Local Government Boards, and later the County and Borough Councils, responsible for the upkeep of the roads. But their hostility to cyclists was slight compared with that which greeted the first motorists in the late 1890s. Motor cars were seen as playthings of the idle rich, and the middle classes who paid most of the rates, complained bitterly about the increasing amount of money being spent on repairing the roads. The motor cars' fast-moving pneumatic tyres sucked out the binding medium from the road surface, so that the clouds of dust raised by each passing car on a dry day were seen as evidence of the damage being done to the road. The water carts with sprinkler bars across the back which had long been used to lay the dust in an age of slower, heavier traffic, proved quite inadequate to deal with the problem.

The worst sufferers were the motorists themselves, for whom the dust was not only unpleasant but dangerous, for it could temporarily blind the driver. Protective helmets, goggles and leather coats were obligatory, and any lady hardy enough to be a passenger travelled with her head and face swathed in long, thick veils.

In April 1900 the Automobile Club (now the Royal Automobile Club) organised a 1000-mile, three-week tour of Britain with the object of promoting automobilism in this country and showing what these vehicles could do over long distances and in hilly country. There were over 80 entries of various sizes and capacity, including motor tricycles, steam-powered models, and the most elaborate Napiers, Daimlers, Panhards and other makes. The start took place at 7 a.m. on 23 April, when the extraordinary procession set out from Hyde Park Corner and made its way along the Bath Road through Hounslow and Maidenhead to Reading. Hundreds of cyclists accompanied them, and people turned out in towns and villages along the route to watch them go by.

They had been timed to arrive in Reading just after 10.30, but many arrived as much as an hour earlier. Three miles west of the town they turned off the road into the drive of Calcot Park, where they were entertained to a magnificent champagne breakfast in a marquee at the back of the house by Mr Alfred Harmsworth (later Lord Northcliffe), the newspaper magnate, who was himself a keen motorist. After breakfast, the motorists continued on their way through Newbury, Calne and Chippenham to Bristol, the end of the first day's trip, where, as at other major towns and cities on the route, the cars were lined up for exhibition to the public.

Although it was claimed that some of the cars were capable of reaching a speed of 40 miles an hour the authorities had insisted that the trial must not be a race, and speed limits of 12 m.p.h. in England and 10 in Scotland had been imposed, reduced to 8 when passing through towns. Policemen were stationed at milestones along the route, checking the times and numbers of the cars as they passed, but although the speed limits were exceeded in places, no drivers were warned or names taken.

The weather on that first day was gloriously fine, the roads consequently at their dustiest, and the press commented on the appalling state of the motorists and their vehicles. During the next few years various sprays were tried out to lay the dust and a decision was eventually made in favour of tar. From 1908 tar spraying proceeded quickly on all main roads, the Bath Road being among the first treated, and that year saw a spectacular change when the old white road was turned to black. It proved an expensive operation. In 1909 the County Surveyor of Berkshire reported that the Bath Road across the county continued to absorb very large quantities of materials, the amount allowed being hardly enough to repair the road and keep pace with the wear and tear of increasingly heavy traffic. The dust problem, however, was solved. In the following year the same Surveyor reported that, of the 31 wells serving the water pumps beside the Bath Road, only three were still in use, although 16 others could give a satisfactory supply of water if put in order. The expense of restoring them and of putting new wooden covers over the wells was considered too great, and it was decided to cover them in with stone slabs.

Automobilism, as the Automobile Club had confidently predicted in 1900, had come to stay. Motor cars were soon joined on the roads by motor buses, which followed the traditional routes of the carriers and short-stage coaches to serve local needs. After World War I, bus fleets were expanded and routes extended rapidly, so that road transport began seriously to rival rail transport. The ever-growing volume of traffic made necessary various alterations to the Bath Road, particularly at the busier eastern end. In the 1920s a major improvement scheme was carried out between Maidenhead Thicket and Reading, which included new stretches of road bypassing Twyford and part of Sonning. Longford and Colnbrook were also bypassed, while through the London suburbs the Great West Road was built to carry traffic past the congested main streets of Brentford and Hounslow. In the 1930s other improvements were made to the road west of Reading. In 1936, under the Ministry of Transport's road classification scheme, the Bath Road was designated a trunk road − a national highway for through traffic − from London to Bath, Bristol and Avonmouth; and the Ministry was to be responsible for its maintenance. In taking on this important role, the road lost its historic name, and has since been known officially as A4.

After World War II, traffic increased to such an extent that it was soon obvious that occasional bypasses and lengths of dual carriageway would not be sufficient to keep the traffic moving. Between the improved sections of road, many towns and villages continued to restrict the flow, while in those places the residents were made to suffer abominably from the noise, fumes, vibrations and dangers of a stream of vehicles which never ceased by day or night. Main streets which had once been centres of local life and trade had become impassable barriers cutting off one side of a village or residential area from the other.

In the mid 1950s plans were put forward for a motorway from London to Bristol and South Wales. An early stage of this was the Maidenhead Bypass, opened in 1961. By 1967 twenty miles of motorway had been completed at the eastern end and 35 miles at the western end, but between Holyport in the east and Tormarton in the west there remained a gap of 78 miles which, because of the strength of the opposition put up against it, was not bridged for another four years. Landowners, racehorse trainers, farmers, archaeologists and various countryside protection societies, all protested against the construction of a motorway across some of the most beautiful and historic parts of Berkshire and Wiltshire, and every proposed route and section of route was the subject of enquiries and revisions.

Meanwhile A4 was suffering from gruelling years of overuse. A traffic census taken in July 1970 counted 30,000 vehicles a day on the road between Maidenhead Thicket and Reading, whereas its design capacity was for about 13,000. The result was chaos, with traffic jams at peak morning and evening hours stretching back ten miles east of the notorious bottleneck at Reading. At Newbury a relief road had been opened in 1965, moving the A4 traffic a little further from the town centre, but the problems caused by the junction of A4 with A34, from the Midlands to Southampton, were as bad as ever. At Hungerford, Marlborough, Calne and Chippenham, main streets were continually blocked by a slow-moving stream of traffic, reduced to a standstill when huge heavy lorries negotiated sharp bends between long-suffering buildings. Fortunately by 1970 the line of the motorway had, at last, been agreed and construction was in progress.

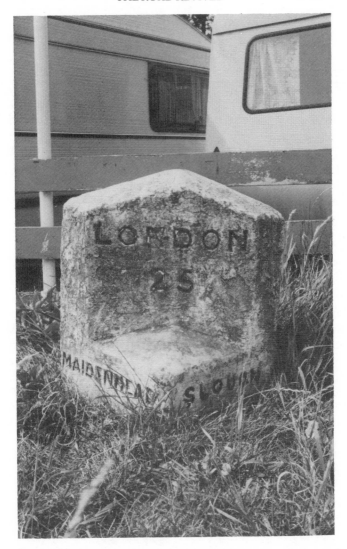

A milestone, almost completely buried, alongside the modern A4 near Slough

The M4 was opened throughout its length on 22 December 1971.

M4 passes well to the north of Bath, and avoids also every other town and village which lay on the Bath Road, and whose inns and tradesmen were vital to the people who travelled along it. On the motorway, rare service stations fulfil the functions of all those places. Since 1971 M4 has relieved A4 of all heavy and long-distance traffic, and A4, as official jargon puts it, has been 'de-trunked'. But it is still a very busy road, crowded with local traffic.

A4 overlays the Bath Road for most of its length, and parts of it have been so heavily used, and so altered, during the last half-century that relics of its past history are becoming increasingly hard to find. Near London almost nothing survives, and sprawling developments have created such devastation and ugliness that, even by the 1930s, the Great West Road had been nicknamed the Great Worst Road. After World War II the expansion of London Airport at Heathrow, built over much of the area of Hounslow Heath, brought its own huge increase of traffic, and caused the destruction of many more old inns and historic landmarks. A few miles further west, in Slough, it is hard to believe, when looking at the untidy mound at Salt Hill, that this was where the Eton Montem ceremony took place, and that near here were two of the finest inns on the Bath Road, the Castle and the Windmill, both possessing beautiful gardens.

Where bypasses have been built, and A4 drives straight ahead, the Bath Road can be followed as it meanders quietly through Longford, Colnbrook, Twyford, Theale or Speen. It is in such places that reminders of the past can be found – the road itself, often surprisingly narrow and winding; the remains of cast iron pumps; weathered milestones; old houses dating from a more gracious age, and ancient inns still in business, although bereft of the stable-yards and coach-houses which once lay behind them. In towns such as Maidenhead, Reading and Newbury, the demands of progress have swept away nearly all signs of the coaching age, and the great inns – the Sun, the Crown, the Bear, the Pelican, and many others – no longer present their tall, many-windowed fronts to the former route of the Bath Road.

The Bath Road, now the A4, passing through Wiltshire today

Further west the road becomes more rural, as it has always done, and Marlborough, Calne, Chippenham and Devizes are less drastically changed. Between these towns the A4 keeps more closely to the line of the Bath Road, and winds smoothly and pleasantly up and down hills which appear never to have been rugged or steep. Driving easily along, it is difficult for the motorist to imagine the struggles and strains of the old-time travellers, as they plodded stoically through the mud, fought against the storms on Cherhill Hill, or jolted perilously down the rocky road into Marlborough. Only by leaving the modern road, to seek out the Old Bath Road still making its way over Beacon Hill, is it possible to see something of the hardships of those days. Standing where the turnpike gate used to be, near Heddington, and the broad track climbs up towards the lonely, rugged heights, it is easier to imagine the sound of iron-shod wheels in stony ruts, the creak and jingle of harness as horses strain to haul a heavy coach onwards, and to see when they have passed through, the gate-keeper return to the warmth of his cottage, and shut the door upon the windy night.

Index